BLESSINGS FOR WOMEN

BLESSINGS FOR WOMEN

100 Assurances of God's Enduring Love

Anna Haggard

Our Daily Bread
Publishing.

Blessings for Women: 100 Assurances of God's Enduring Love
© 2025 by Our Daily Bread Publishing

Bible permissions statements can be found on the last page.

Interior design by Patti Brinks

ISBN,978-1-916718-52-4

Printed in the United Kingdom
25 26 27 28 29 30 31 32 / 8 7 6 5 4 3 2 1

Contents

DAY 1

God Is Attentive to You

Can a mother forget the baby at her breast
　　　and have no compassion on the child she has
　　　　　borne?
Though she may forget,
　　　I will not forget you! (Isaiah 49:15)

• •

Nothing is outside of God's sight or escapes his notice.

Whatever your journey or wherever you are, know that God is intimately aware of your every joy, heartache, and fear. Rest assured—he is near.

May you lift your eyes toward him, because his gaze is directed on you in care and compassion.

May you listen to his voice, because his ears are attuned to your silent prayers.

May you trust that your heavenly Father is intimately involved with—and tenderly caring for—every detail of your life.

He hasn't forgotten you. And he never will.

Trust him when he says that he's working on your behalf.

Jesus, help me know that nothing escapes your notice or your attention. Show me how much you love me, that I'm always on your mind.

DAY 2

Woman of Valor, Rise Up!

W ho can find a [*hayil* woman]?
   She is more precious than rubies.
      (Proverbs 31:10 NLT)

Those who hope in the LORD
   will renew their strength.
They will soar on wings like eagles;
   they will run and not grow weary,
they will walk and not be faint. (Isaiah 40:31)

• •

WOMAN OF VALOR. In Proverbs 31:10, the author asks, "Who can find a [*hayil* woman]? She is more precious than rubies." Though often translated as "noble," "virtuous," "excellent," or "good" in verse 10, *hayil* is most frequently rendered "valiant" in the Bible, and that seems a more fitting translation here. *Hayil* most often describes military strength, the courage and force of elite warriors (Joshua 10:7). The word even describes the limitless power of God himself (Habakkuk 3:19). As you read these blessings, may you embrace your Christ-given identity and strength as a *hayil* woman—a woman of valor.

• •

O woman of valor, rise up!
Do not lose courage, heart, or hope but instead soar—

Now is the time to take flight—
Now is the time to awaken your joy,
to throw off fear
and to wait expectantly on God.

O woman of valor, rise up!
Strengthen your arms for the work that lies ahead:
May you lengthen and widen, spread to the right and
to the left, and stake the kingdom territory God has
called you to possess.
May the overflowing power of God's Spirit pour out to uplift
and to bless those you love.

Take hold of the peace and deep joy that is already yours in
Christ.

O woman of valor, rise up!
May you be a well-watered garden:
May you plant your roots
deep in the soil of God's presence, faithfulness, and love.
Do not retreat, but in reverence, kneel.
O woman of valor, take courage:
May you discover your weakness is power at Jesus's feet.

*Jesus, in these days of confusion and
uncertainty, may I dare to look up and find
strength and power in you and to ready my
heart and mind for the work that lies ahead.*

DAY 3

Blessing Small Beginnings

Do not despise these small beginnings, for the LORD rejoices to see the work begin. (Zechariah 4:10 NLT)

May you not despise the day of small beginnings.

May you not fixate on your setbacks, fears, or failures, but embrace this day with eyes of faith.

Do not lose heart or hope but trust that one day total victory is yours.

In the meantime, pay attention to small breakthroughs and ordinary blessings.

God blesses this day of fresh starts.

Today, press in.

Don't let up or back down.

Look up.

With everything you have, commit to believing that God's strength overcomes your weaknesses, his calming reassurance will soothe your fears, his plans and purposes eclipse your circumstances.

Steadfastly trust that the God who loves you wholeheartedly is orchestrating everything for your highest good.

God of the breakthrough, may I patiently trust that you are in control and that each day of my life is attended to and orchestrated by your loving care and sovereign power.

DAY 4

Lord of Heaven's Armies
(*Yahweh Tsebaoth*)

The nations are in chaos,
　　　and their kingdoms crumble!
God's voice thunders,
　　　and the earth melts!
The LORD of Heaven's Armies is here among us;
　　　the God of Israel is our fortress.　　　*Interlude*

Come, see the glorious works of the LORD:
　　　See how he brings destruction upon the world.
He causes wars to end throughout the earth.
　　　He breaks the bow and snaps the spear;
　　　he burns the shields with fire.

"Be still, and know that I am God!" (Psalm 46:6–10 NLT)

• •

LORD OF HEAVEN'S ARMIES (*Yahweh Tsebaoth*). This name, used more than two hundred times in Scripture, demonstrates God's supremacy over earth, the cosmos, and the spiritual world. Sometimes the Bible names the Lord of Heaven's Armies as the leader of a battalion of angels. The Lord of Heaven's Armies

wages spiritual war and overcomes all things on behalf of his loved ones.

· ·

Amid your maelstrom—whatever your temptation or trial—and no matter the depth of your weariness, you can be still.

You serve the God of Heaven's Armies. He can, and will, unleash the forces of heaven and earth when you pray.

May you lift up your head and call on *Yahweh Tsebaoth*.

May you trust that God will offer you his outsized strength, meet your every need, and lay hold of your enemy.

Some battles are not yours to fight.

Be still and know that he is the God of Heaven's Armies.

Lord of Heaven's Armies, help! I can't face this [circumstance, challenge, or anxiety] on my own. I feel powerless, but I invite you to enter this circumstance and to do battle on my behalf.

DAY 5

Inviting Jesus into Your Weakness

The sacrifices of God are a broken spirit;
a broken and contrite heart, O God, you will not despise. (Psalm 51:17 ESV)

"My grace is sufficient for you, for my power is made perfect in weakness." Therefore I will boast all the more gladly of my weaknesses, so that the power of Christ may rest upon me. (2 Corinthians 12:9 ESV)

• •

May you know that your dependency, your neediness—the things the world despises—are highly precious to God.

When you cry out, Christ immediately responds! May you lay bare your deepest desires before God, and invite him into your longings, sorrows, and joys.

Your vulnerability draws him close to you. God is moved by your heart, he desires to fulfill your dreams and desires, and he longs to tenderly care for you.

Today, may you fully release your limitations and concerns to God and receive his immeasurable wisdom, power, and strength to buoy and sustain you, whatever the circumstances or unknowns you face.

Today, may you exchange your weakness for God's limitless strength.

Jesus, thank you that you aren't repelled or surprised by my weakness—that my neediness draws me closer to you. God, today, please help me with [identify your prayer request]. I am awed and grateful by your help and personal care!

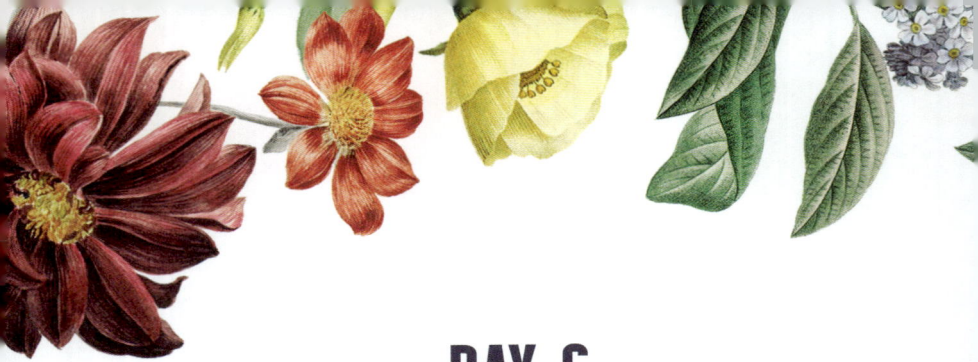

DAY 6

Blessed Is She

And Mary said, "Behold, I am the servant of the Lord; let it be to me according to your word." And the angel departed from her. (Luke 1:38 ESV)

Blessed is she who has believed that the Lord would fulfill his promises to her! (Luke 1:45)

. . . .

Faith is not always the grand gesture, the bold declaration, the leap in the dark.

More often, it's the unspoken *yes*—however timidly made—acknowledged deep within yourself: *to let go of what's behind and receive God's fullness for you now.*

When Mary surrendered herself to God's will and received the world's greatest mission, she simply said yes.

"Let it be to me according to your word." *Let it be to me.*

Whatever your circumstances, may you—as Mary did—entrust your future, your plans, and your will wholeheartedly to God.

Dare to believe God's generosity, knowing that the greatest act of faith can be enclosed in a yes.

Heavenly Father, today I say yes, surrendering my life to you, your timing, and your ways. Help me openly receive your abundant joy and fresh beginnings.

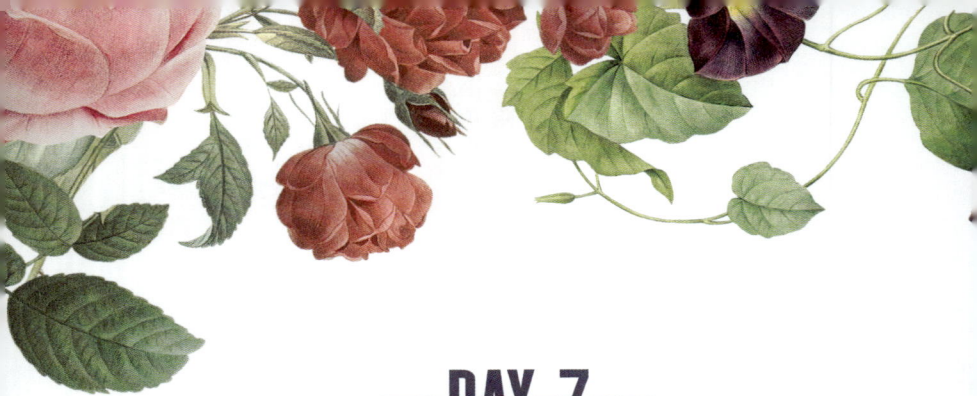

DAY 7

Saying Yes to God

I came that they may have and enjoy life, and have it in abundance [to the full, till it overflows]. (John 10:10 AMP)

- -

May you have the courage to say no so that you can say yes to all that God has for you.

May you let go of what drains, sidetracks, or weakens you and open yourself to life-giving relationships, to uplifting work, to prayer, to creative pursuits, and to God.

May you give sacrificially and love deeply.

May you trade tasks that are not yours to shoulder for the things that only you can do.

May you exchange time-wasters for soul-sustaining, enlivening activities.

May you discover what truly fulfills your heart's longings and enlarges your soul.

God desires to offer you life and to reignite your joy.

Jesus, help me to say yes to what deepens my relationship with you and with those you've given me to love. Thank you for the wondrous gift of life.

DAY 8

Freedom in Surrender

I pray that you, being rooted and established in love, may have power, together with all the Lord's holy people, to grasp how wide and long and high and deep is the love of Christ, and to know this love that surpasses knowledge— that you may be filled to the measure of all the fullness of God. (Ephesians 3:17–19)

. . . .

May your courage and delight in God deepen and widen, brim up and overflow, as you open yourself to the vast, joyous currents of God's deep, deep love.

Dare to encounter the wild goodness of your heavenly Father.

Dare to surrender to God's replenishing healing, freedom, and joy.

Dare to behold the fierceness of his devotion and the unyielding force of his unchanging purposes and passions.

Dare to say yes to responding and receiving God's tender, restorative care instead of remaining firmly in control.

While Christ's love is boundless and untamed, in God you are safe and seen, known and jubilantly loved.

Dare to be amazed and in awe of Love as vast as an ocean.

Heavenly Father, Jesus, and Holy Spirit, let your Love wash over me, free me from my fears, and offer me the peace found in surrender. May I be filled to the measure of all the fullness of God.

DAY 9

Blessing for Your Home

The LORD bless you
    and keep you;
the LORD make his face shine on you
    and be gracious to you;
the LORD turn his face toward you
    and give you peace. (Numbers 6:24–26)

May your home be a place of deep peace,
filled with forgiveness and understanding,
where the sacred but ordinary rhythms of boiling,
simmering, working, laughing, and sleeping meet;
a safe space for asking questions,
for sharing hard things,
for experiencing wonder and joy.

May your home be a place of renewal,
inviting those seeking second chances and fresh starts;
a space where hearts come alive;
where bodies and souls are nourished;
a space where the Spirit can breathe refreshment and life-
giving purpose into lives and spirits.
May your home welcome rest.

Above all, may your home be a place to be known and loved.

*Jesus, may my home be a spacious place
for your presence, leading, and purposes.
May the Holy Spirit's joy, peace, and love be
felt by all who walk through my doors.*

DAY 10

God Almighty (*El Shaddai*)

When Abram was ninety-nine years old, the LORD appeared to him and said, "I am God Almighty; walk before me faithfully. . . . I will make you very fruitful." (Genesis 17:1, 6)

· ·

GOD ALMIGHTY (*El Shaddai*). God revealed this covenant name to Abram when promising him many descendants—even though the ninety-nine-year-old Abram and his octogenarian wife, Sarai, were barren (Genesis 17:1–2). A year later, their son, Isaac, was born. In its context, the name *El Shaddai* reveals that God keeps his promises, no matter how impossible they seem.

· ·

May you trust in God's promises more than your limitations and fears.

You are held by God Almighty. Unbound by time and space, *El Shaddai* is the God of infinite, immeasurable blessings.

Nothing is too hard for God. Everything is under his control.

May you view God's promises as if they were already deposited into your hands. What God Almighty purposes and plans, you can accept and receive in faith as true and real.

May *El Shaddai* unleash the seemingly impossible for you and your loved ones.

God Almighty, nothing is too hard for you.
Whenever I am discouraged, remind me that you
desire to personally bless your loved ones out
of the abundance of your provision and care.

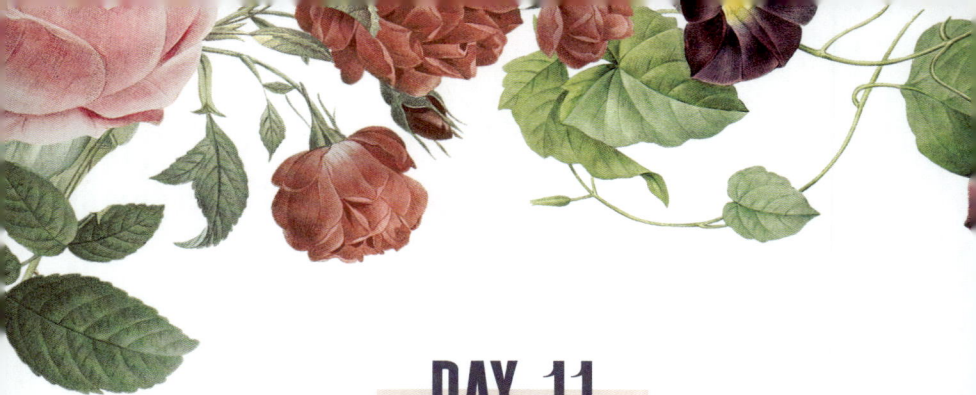

DAY 11

Stop Striving

Commit everything you do to the Lord.
Trust him, and he will help you. (Psalm 37:5 NLT)

May the thing that you've carried for years—the unanswered prayer, the broken relationship, the overwhelming concern—be committed to Jesus's loving care.

Do you hear his gentle whisper to stop striving?

Cease struggling,
let it rest with him.

Whatever the routines and responsibilities of your day, may you completely release that burden into his everlasting arms. May God quiet your fears as you enter this place of rest.

Be reassured: your Comforter, Provider, and Sustainer is intimately involved with and will care for you and your situation. His ways are beyond your own.

You are surrounded on all sides by the shield of his love and protection.

God, I commit [my situation, relationship, concern] to you. Today, help me to let go of this heavy burden and entrust it to your loving care, knowing that your wisdom and your ways are higher than my own.

DAY 12

Under God's Wings

He will cover you with his feathers,
  and under his wings you will find refuge;
    his faithfulness will be your shield and rampart.
      (Psalm 91:4)

May the LORD repay you for what you have done. May you be richly rewarded by the LORD, the God of Israel, under whose wings you have come to take refuge. (Ruth 2:12)

· ·

May you hide yourself in God, knowing that under his wings is the safest space to be.

May you come to him in vulnerability, in weakness, in trust—in need—knowing that he'll embrace you right there.

Here, under the refuge of his wings—nourished with wisdom, fed inexhaustible strength, sheltered by compassion—you are completely safe.

Here, you are wholly protected from the enemy.

Here, you can find deep fulfillment, nurturing care, and joy—nourishment for your mind, body, and soul.

In God's safe, wild presence, discover the maternal side of God, that, like an eagle, is attentive, far-seeing—fierce.

God's love for you cannot be tamed.

Jesus, thank you for the protection found under the refuge of your wings. Give me awareness of your nurturing, maternal presence, and open me to the assurances of your love.

DAY 13

Invitation to Reset

Whatever is true, whatever is noble, whatever is right, whatever is pure, whatever is lovely, whatever is admirable—if anything is excellent or praiseworthy—think about such things. Whatever you have learned or received or heard from me, or seen in me—put it into practice. And the God of peace will be with you. (Philippians 4:8–9)

Each day offers an invitation for a reset.

Whatever yesterday's decisions or mistakes, choose today to fasten your mind to what is true and beautiful instead of what will diminish, drain, or distract you.

May you ponder that which will shape you, not break you.

May you engage in practices that make you spiritually alive and emotionally whole.

May you discern between habits that help you temporarily escape discomfort from those that offer you true peace and lasting rest for your soul.

May you consume less of what causes you anxiety, fear, and confusion, and instead choose pursuits that make you come alive.

Today, may you reset your mind for the renewal of your whole self.

Jesus, today presents an overwhelming amount of options for how I can spend my time. Help me choose what brings lasting peace and draws me closer to you.

DAY 14

Being God's Beloved

Blessed and worthy of praise be the God and Father of our Lord Jesus Christ, who has blessed us with every spiritual blessing in the heavenly realms in Christ, just as [in His love] He chose us in Christ [actually selected us for Himself as His own] before the foundation of the world, so that we would be holy [that is, consecrated, set apart for Him, purpose-driven] and blameless in His sight. (Ephesians 1: 3–4 AMP)

. . . .

Today, make room—widen the space!—for your *belovedness* in Christ.

It's time to let the radiant light of this everlasting truth pour into the open windows of your heart, mind, and soul—in Christ, you are more than enough.

Experience the reassuring joy and safety of being seen, heard, and known in God's presence and receive His comforting assurance that He pursues you in love and listens to your every prayer.

Even as you face unanswered prayers, self-doubt, and uncertainty about your worthiness, may you listen to God in the deepest part of your being: you are safely grounded in God's Love for all eternity, chosen by Him to possess the unchanging status of beloved before the foundation of the world.

Take heart: you are safe, held, and eternally protected by God.

Beloved, you are God's, and God is yours, for all eternity.

Jesus, you are infinite, unrivaled, and majestic, and yet you call me yours, and you are mine. Let this wondrous truth release me for a life of faith and fresh courage to follow wherever you lead me.

DAY 15

A Straight Path

I will guide you along the best pathway for your life.
　　I will advise you and watch over you.
　　　　(Psalm 32:8 NLT)

Whatever your unknowns or worries, your future is in God's loving hands.

In your journey ahead, may your heavenly Father shield and protect you on all sides. May the Spirit anticipate your every need and open the way before you. May Christ safeguard your every step.

May the Father, Son, and Spirit refresh your vision and comfort and reassure you.

May they not only sustain you and keep you but allow for the winds of renewal and rest to fall afresh and gently carry you along your journey.

Whatever lies ahead, may you have the unwavering assurance that God will lead you along the best pathways for your life.

Take courage: God promises to make your way straight.

Father, Son, and Holy Spirit, you hold the keys to all power, wisdom, and provision, and I trust you to direct me on the best pathways for my life.

DAY 16

For Seasons of Waiting

But blessed is the one who trusts in the LORD,
>   whose confidence is in him.
They will be like a tree planted by the water
>   that sends out its roots by the stream.
It does not fear when heat comes;
>   its leaves are always green.
It has no worries in a year of drought
>   and never fails to bear fruit. (Jeremiah 17:7–8)

· ·

When you're in a wilderness—a space of unanswered prayers, of disappointments, of discouragement, of doubt, and of fear . . .

May you know that God hears you.

Even in the heat, your Shepherd guides you safely to shelter, and keeps you fed, nourished, and protected.

No time is ever wasted—no wilderness too barren to be forgotten by God.

May springs of replenishment, healing, and deep joy overflow in your desert, because, at all times, your Comforter and Sustainer walks by your side. He is your Shade in the heat, your Sustenance in a scorched wasteland, your Protector in your dark night.

In the deepest part of you, trust that—even in your wilderness—God watches over you. Take courage that God promises to provide for your every need out of his immense care and unlimited resources.

In dry, unexpected places, may you encounter the abundance of God's healing and the protection of his profound peace.

God, even in my seasons of waiting, may I experience your goodness, your presence, and your overflowing kindness to me.

DAY 17

The God Who Sees Me (*El Roi*)

She [Hagar] gave this name to the LORD who spoke to her: "You are the God who sees me," for she said, "I have now seen the One who sees me." (Genesis 16:13)

THE GOD WHO SEES ME (*El Roi*). Abandoned and abused, the enslaved woman Hagar addressed God as *El Roi*, "the God who sees me," after encountering him in the wilderness (Genesis 16:13). Attending to Hagar's desperate situation, God provided Hagar and her unborn son, Ishmael, promises of hope and blessing.

In the areas where you feel rejected, broken, or betrayed, may you know that God sees you. God isn't absent from your pain.

He hears you. He knows your heart's cry. He is present in your suffering.

May you turn your eyes from your present confusion to the One who binds up your wounds, restores, and makes you whole.

El Roi calls you his own. May he bind and heal, restore and renew you: mind, body, and soul.

May God remake what was intended for evil into that which becomes your highest good.

El Roi, *you are the God who sees me. Help me remember that, no matter what, I am held in the embrace of your loving gaze. Please heal the broken and wounded places in me.*

DAY 18

Dependent on Him

But he said to me, "My grace is sufficient for you, for my power is made perfect in weakness." Therefore I will boast all the more gladly about my weaknesses, so that Christ's power may rest on me. . . . For when I am weak, then I am strong. (2 Corinthians 12:9–10)

· ·

You are more powerful than you know.

No matter your failures, inadequacies, or sins, God opens wide his arms to you, inviting you to take refuge in him alone.

As you rely on God's power, may you find courage in the areas that once held you captive.

As you stand on Christ's promises, may you triumph where you previously faltered.

As you abide in his presence, may you exchange your weakness for his infinite strength.

May God's tender, everlasting commitment to you strengthen your heart, uplift your spirit, and revive your faith.

You are completely safe and secure in God's love.

God, I know that my weakness is strength when I depend on you. Thank you for your everlasting commitment to me and for the power you've given me to overcome my every trial.

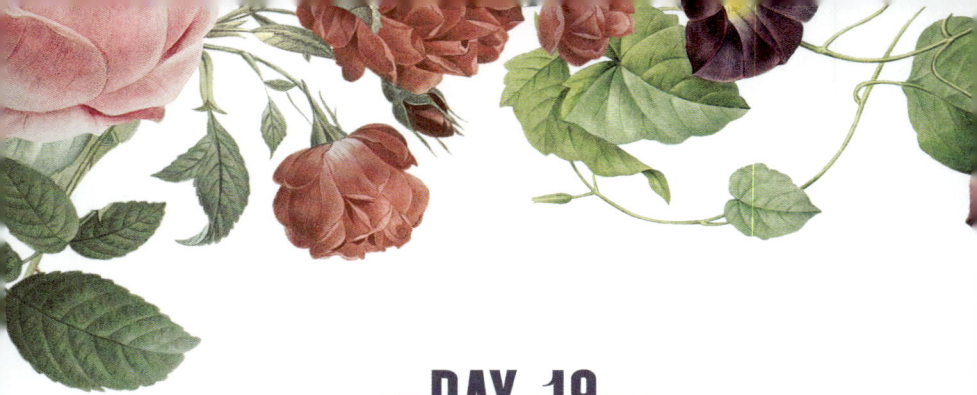

DAY 19

Doing the Next Right Thing

The way of the righteous is like the first gleam of dawn, which shines ever brighter until the full light of day. (Proverbs 4:18 NLT)

Allow God to guide you through this day.

In seasons when you're waiting for prayers to be answered, dreams to be realized, relationships to be restored, still know that God is at your side. He hasn't abandoned or left you to navigate the situation, relationship, or anxiety on your own.

Trust—have confident expectation—that he will provide an answer in due time.

Meanwhile, focus on doing the next right thing, whether that is:

Eating a healthy meal
Taking a walk

Tackling the task at hand
Reaching out to someone

Above all else, know this—you can trust him with the things and people most precious to you.

God, you care more about my concerns than I do. Help me to transfer the weight of my circumstances, cares, and worries to your strong shoulders, and in the waiting, deepen my trust that you are working out all things for good—for my loved ones and me.

DAY 20

Groundswell of God's Love

The LORD makes firm the steps
of the one who delights in him;
though he may stumble, he will not fall,
for the LORD upholds him with his hand.
(Psalm 37:23–24)

You are safe to dare, dream, and risk.

Even when you feel uncertain or hesitant, go out and try anyway.

You are upheld by the groundswell of God's never-ending love.

When you risk and fail, even when you waver,
you ultimately cannot fall, knowing you are carried by the protective love of God's outstretched hand.

Even when you're afraid, keep showing up.

God doesn't care how uneven, ugly, or unpolished your journey appears from the outside. May you take heart that God sees you as you truly are. Christ delights in your committed decision to undertake the slow, laborious process of being refinished, refined, and remade by the awesome power of his immense grace and love.

Whatever your mistakes, trust that God is exceedingly pleased with you.

God, you are the One who truly sees me as I am. You free me to risk and try new things, knowing that I am surrounded and protected by your love and limitless grace.

DAY 21

Doing Today's Tasks with God

Cast all your anxiety on him because he cares for you. (1 Peter 5:7)

• •

May you give today's tasks, cares, and concerns to God—entrusting each one to his sovereign, all-wise, and all-loving care.

Take comfort: this day is not yours, but his. God holds your situation securely. Everything about this day is under his limitless authority, and he is able to meet your every need.

When working in tandem with him, the task that is unmanageable can become lighter.

The one that is impossible, made possible.

That burden, when taken on with him, will be overcome instead of overcoming you.

Whatever your challenge—and however inadequate you feel in meeting it—pause and remember . . .

God had made this day, and he made you—and nothing about it or you (or your perceived inadequacies) surprises him.

He will carry you through.

Trust him.

God, I trust that my weaknesses can be carried through your limitless strength, mercy, and love. Thank you for collaborating with me in rising to meet every responsibility or struggle this day brings.

DAY 22

Adventure Ahead

You care for the land and water it;
    you enrich it abundantly.
The streams of God are filled with water
    to provide the people with grain,
    for so you have ordained it.
You drench its furrows and level its ridges;
    you soften it with showers and bless its crops.
    (Psalm 65:9–10)

. . . .

May you view this day through the eyes of adventure.

May you watch for opportunities to feel gratitude and awe for unexpected gifts and hidden blessings.

Savor quiet moments.

May you embrace the joy of belonging to God.

Behold the sacred and exquisite in the ordinary rhythms of life.

Have fun (and let go!).

Lean into God's everlasting arms. Taste God's goodness. Encounter his deep peace.

Feel a sense of deep wonder for all that you possess in God.

Jesus, give me eyes to see the sacred and ordinary gifts you provide each day. Thank you for your daily blessings and your moment-by-moment faithfulness to me.

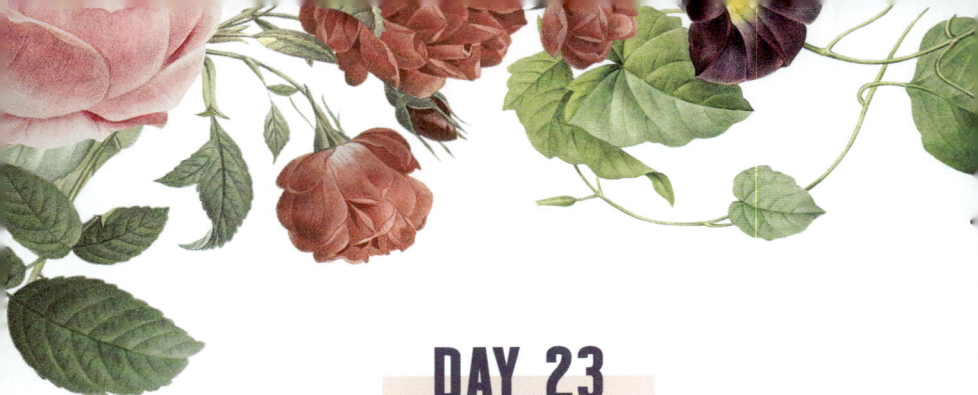

DAY 23

Jealous God (*El Kanna*)

You must worship no other gods, for the LORD, whose very name is Jealous, is a God who is jealous about his relationship with you. (Exodus 34:14 NLT)

· ·

JEALOUS GOD (*El Kanna*). In the wilderness, God revealed himself to the Israelites as *El Kanna*, "Jealous God" (Exodus 34:14). In the Ten Commandments, God decreed the Israelites worship no other gods, because Yahweh—like a faithful husband—desired an exclusive relationship with his people. Likewise, out of his devotion and unwavering commitment to you, *El Kanna* will not tolerate any rivals competing for your love and worship.

· ·

God is jealous for you.

May *El Kanna* be your first love.

May you turn your eyes from what ensnares your heart, captures your imagination, and distracts you from passionately giving yourself to God, and turn to him with undivided attention, praise, and devotion.

May you fill yourself up with his perfect, everlasting love. Whatever season you're in, may you seek to please *El Kanna* above all others.

May you delight yourself in the storehouse of his provision and take joy in his many gifts. But amid your abundance, may you never forget to turn your eyes to the Source of your every blessing.

You are loved by God with a relentless, reckless—jealous—love.

May you be forever mesmerized by him.

El Kanna, *I'm in awe of, and deeply grateful for, your devotion to me. Search my heart and bring to mind anything I've prioritized over you.*

DAY 24

Hearing God's Gentle Whisper

After the earthquake came a fire, but the LORD was not in the fire. And after the fire came a gentle whisper. (1 Kings 19:12)

. . . .

May you risk listening to God's still, small voice amidst the ruckus and relentless distractions of culture.

May you make way for God's healing and breakthrough by offering him a spacious place to move freely and work mightily in your life.

May you let go of your addictions for control and certainty to free yourself up for surrendering completely to the trustworthy God who cares for you and is sovereign over everything.

May your desire to please others lose its hold over you as God's favor and opinion increase in worth in your eyes.

May you feel the depth of God's delight as he draws ever closer to you in love.

May you know that you move God's heart when you pray.

Heavenly Father, no matter the chaos and confusion around me, deepen my faith and trust in your goodness and care for me.

Living Wisely and Discerning the Time

There is a time for everything,
 and a season for every activity under the heavens:

>   a time to be born and a time to die,
>   a time to plant and a time to uproot,
>   a time to kill and a time to heal,
>   a time to tear down and a time to build,
>   a time to weep and a time to laugh,
>   a time to mourn and a time to dance,
>   a time to scatter stones and a time to gather them,
>   a time to embrace and a time to refrain from
>   embracing,
>   a time to search and a time to give up,
>   a time to keep and a time to throw away,
>   a time to tear and a time to mend,
>   a time to be silent and a time to speak,
>   a time to love and a time to hate,
>   a time for war and a time for peace.
>   (Ecclesiastes 3:1–8)

May you be wise to discern the times in which you live and the choices that present themselves to you.

May you have the courage to plant, but may you also risk uprooting when you've outgrown your space.

May you mend fences and build bridges, but also discern the time to retreat for healing and healthy boundaries.

In your trials, may you honor your grief and heartache, and may you retain a lifelong sense of wonder and curiosity at the joys life brings.

May you dare to rise up when the world needs you to raise your voice.

But may you risk being still when it's time to quiet yourself and remember that the Lord is God.

Eternal God, in this season and time of my life, help me to live wisely and according to your ways. Teach me to be sensitive to your voice and to seek your direction and guidance daily.

DAY 26

Refreshment for Today

G ive thanks to the LORD, for he is good;
    his love endures forever. (Psalm 118:29)

May you live joyfully and wholeheartedly.

May you dare to explore and take risks, no matter how small.

May you look at this day with awakened gratitude and fresh faith.

Anticipate the crisp, cool refreshment of surprise.

Each day, God delights in you and desires to fill you with joy overflowing.

You possess an eternal hope and a glorious future with him.

In the meantime, God invites you to stop and enjoy all the luminous treasures along the way.

Jesus, help me pay attention to each day's delights. Thank you for being the source of every good thing.

DAY 27

For Days of Uncertainty and Adversity

Even though I walk
     through the darkest valley,
I will fear no evil,
     for you are with me;
your rod and your staff,
     they comfort me. (Psalm 23:4)

He guides me along the right paths. (Psalm 23:3)

May you know that however dark the night, however incomprehensible the way, you are never alone.

Even when you can't sense his presence, may you trust that God has never left your side.

God walks with you, gently guiding you in the dark, preventing you from becoming entangled by the snares and dangers along the road.

May you press in to him—clinging to his faithfulness and lovingkindness

until your dawn breaks.

God, when my vision is clouded, and my circumstances are disorienting, you take hold of my hand. Help me entrust myself— and the uncertainties of my journey—to your safekeeping and loving care.

DAY 28

When You Miss the Mark

Though the righteous fall seven times, they rise again. (Proverbs 24:16)

May you get back up again when you've lost your footing.

No matter how disorienting or adverse your circumstances, may you cling to God and his Word. Whatever challenges you face, God's loving compassion for you will never fail, falter, or change.

God sees you through the eyes of boundless grace and mercy. In your confusion and need, your loving Father offers you his hand.

Jesus doesn't come to condemn but to pull you back on your feet.

Jesus, you graciously hold my fears and shame, cover me with your mercy and compassion, and gaze at me through eyes of grace. Thank you for loving me just as I am.

DAY 29

When You Feel Discouraged

Though [God] brings grief, he will show compassion, so great is his unfailing love. (Lamentations 3:32)

Nothing will be impossible with God. (Luke 1:37 ESV)

· ·

May you be gentle with the space inside yourself that feels empty from losses and disappointments: of possibilities that at one time seemed bright, promising—assured—left unfulfilled.

May you know that God honors your unflinching honesty: to see things as they are, instead of wishing for what might have been.

While you cannot change the past, God isn't finished working things out in your present. Nothing in your life is wasted. No matter your circumstances, he holds your pain and sorrow close to his heart, and you can trust that your Comforter is still orchestrating your future for your good and his glory.

Nothing is impossible with God.

God, hold me in this season of grief and heartache. Renew my hope and restore my vision so I can believe that you are in the process of making all things new.

DAY 30

In the Light of His Love

Who can understand his errors?
Cleanse me from secret faults.
Keep back Your servant also from presumptuous sins;
Let them not have dominion over me.
Then I shall be blameless,
And I shall be innocent of great transgression.
(Psalm 19:12–13 NKJV)

. . . .

May those secret sins you carry—some hidden even from yourself—be brought to his gentle light.

In the light of his presence, they can be aired out, cleansed—healed.

Only in the dark do they have unfettered dominion over you.

May the sins you're aware of—those sins you've struggled with for years—begin to lose their power as you soak in the light of his presence.

May the radiance of his love break down their strangling influence of fear, shame, and bondage—until they become the fertile soil through which you see the expansion of his immeasurable grace and forgiveness in your life.

Whatever it is that you carry, however secret or acknowledged, know that you can entrust it to the light of his mercy and love for the healing and renewal of your whole self.

Father, thank you for the healing, restorative light of your love. Make known to me the areas of my life that need to be cleansed and renewed, and let me bring them to the light of your gentle, rejuvenating presence.

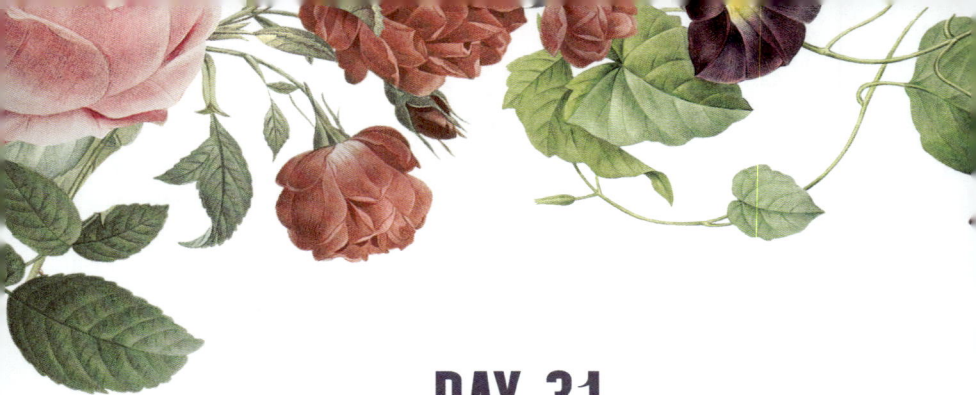

DAY 31

Joy in the Restoration

Then I [Nehemiah] said to them, "You see the trouble we are in: Jerusalem lies in ruins, and its gates have been burned with fire. Come, let us rebuild the wall of Jerusalem, and we will no longer be in disgrace." I also told them about the gracious hand of my God on me and what the king had said to me.

They replied, "Let us start rebuilding." So they began this good work. (Nehemiah 2:17–18)

May you not despise the day of small beginnings.

Focus not on your problems but press in: now is the time to rebuild.

Let go of your fears, throw off your failures, and—with eyes of faith—break ground!

What has been lying desolate—in ruins—in your life, God wants to restore and reclaim.

What God enables you to start, he will remain faithful to help you to finish.

May you lay hold of the joy of this new day. Press in to all that God has promised.

God, thank you that you do not despise small beginnings. Help me to faithfully steward the responsibilities and purposes you have entrusted to me.

DAY 32

Written on the Palm of God's Hand

You saw me before I was born.
    Every day of my life was recorded in your book.
Every moment was laid out
    before a single day had passed. (Psalm 139:16 NLT)

• •

Beloved, may you know that—whatever you do—you can never escape God's lasting commitment and loving care.

Your name is written on the palm of your Abba's hand. He intuits your every thought. Your heavenly Father knows your secret worries, your hidden fears, and your silent heartaches. Even the hairs on your head he has memorized.

Your heavenly Father watches each stage of your life unfold and guards and protects each moment. He who has recorded every day of your life in his book has staked out your future for your glorious good.

May you know that he promises to carry you every step of the way. You are sheltered in his protective, ever-faithful love.

Abba Father, thank you for your attentive, ever-present love and care. I can never escape your love for me. Help me understand just how securely I am held, nurtured, and protected by you.

DAY 33

Making Peace with Being Human

He knows how we are formed,
    he remembers that we are dust. . . .
But from everlasting to everlasting
    the LORD's love is with those who fear him.
      (Psalm 103:14, 17)

May you make peace with being human.
God knows your frailties, and he is pleased with you still.

May you rejoice in your limits, weaknesses, and needs—
because they enable you to turn to the limitless God, in
whom you can do all things.

May you accept the things beyond your control—
giving your future to the One who created eternity and who
intimately cares for your destiny.

Lift up your eyes. Entrust yourself to the One who holds
everything—your sorrows, fears, and joys—in the palm of his
hands.

May you reframe your uncertainties as circumstances held safe and secure in God.

May you give yourself compassion, because your heavenly Father has so much compassion for you.

Heavenly Father, I am only human. Help me to accept my limits, knowing that your grace is sufficient for me. May my weakness be transformed into strength and power in and through you.

DAY 34

Look Up

Lift up your eyes and look to the heavens:
    Who created all these?
He who brings out the starry host one by one
    and calls forth each of them by name.
Because of his great power and mighty strength,
    not one of them is missing. (Isaiah 40:26)

May you go about your day today with a hopeful heart, remembering that your Helper just happens to be Creator of heaven and earth.

In your moments of discouragement and fear, may you look up. He who loves you with an everlasting love also strung the stars together, set the planets in motion, and remembers and names each star in the cosmos.

Everything is under his sovereignty and care. Nothing is impossible with him.

Let him walk with you today. Take hold of his hand. Entrust your whole self to him.

Know this: he will direct you on the right paths. He is able even—and especially—when you aren't.

Jesus, Creator of heaven and earth, you are infinitely able even when I'm weak and inadequate. In my moments of anxiety and discouragement, remind me that everything is under your loving care and that nothing about my life escapes your notice.

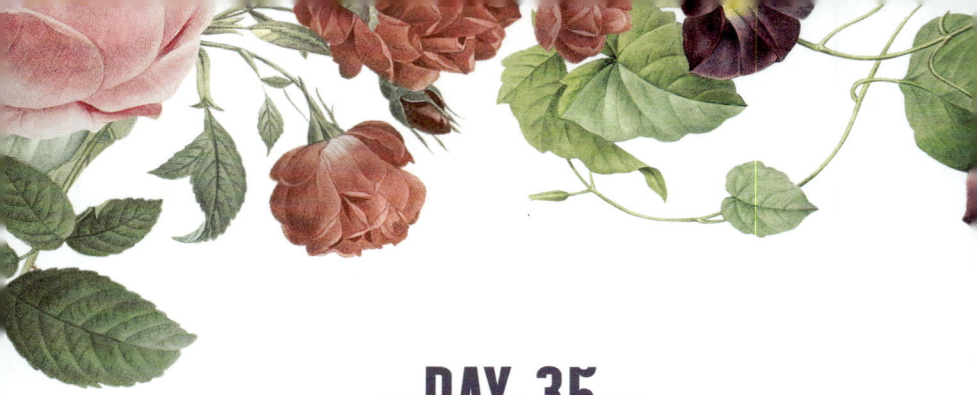

DAY 35

The Lord Will Provide
(*Yahweh Yireh*)

Abraham looked up and there in a thicket he saw a ram caught by its horns. He went over and took the ram and sacrificed it as a burnt offering instead of his son. So Abraham called that place The LORD Will Provide. And to this day it is said, "On the mountain of the LORD it will be provided." (Genesis 22:13–14)

· ·

THE LORD WILL PROVIDE (*Yahweh Yireh*). After testing Abraham, God miraculously provided for him, so Abraham ascribed to God the name *Yahweh Yireh*, "The Lord Will Provide" (Genesis 22). *Yireh* means "provision." It comes from the Hebrew root meaning to "see." In Scripture, the mention of God's sight is often the precursor to his miraculous actions on behalf of his loved ones.

· ·

May the God who holds the knowledge of your future in the palm of his hand, who is working everything out for your good—

who desires your very best—

be your *Yahweh Yireh*, your Great Provider.

May you anticipate the fresh release of his blessings and the breaking through of his mighty power.

Until then—when your circumstances don't match his promises, and when obstacles stir up your fears—may you lay hold of faith and

may you offer God the precious gift of your trust.

Behold how, at just the right time, God will wondrously and unexpectedly break through for you.

Wait on him.

Yahweh Yireh, you supply everything I need out of your infinite resources and incomparable provision. Help me to wait expectantly on you, even when the answers to my prayers remain outside of my vision.

DAY 36

Here, You Are Safe

How often I have longed to gather your children together, as a hen gathers her chicks under her wings. (Matthew 23:37)

On days you are weary, may you hide yourself under the shelter of God's wings—knowing that's where your heavenly Father longs for you to be.

Nestled under God's winged protection, you are in a safe, infinitely secure space.

Here, it's just you and him. Surrender yourself to being enveloped by the peace of God's powerful, protective presence. You don't need to be in control or have it all together. You are invited to relax.

Lean against him. Let go. Rest. Be playful.

Be childlike.

There's no need to be vigilant, guarded, at attention. Briefly forget about being responsible for anyone or anything as you are gathered under God's protective love and grace.

Let the immensity of God's maternal kindness quiet your soul and free your spirit as you put your hope in him.

Father, no matter what is going on around me, help me hide myself under the safety of your love and, with abandon, surround myself with the security of your nurture, comfort, and reassurance.

DAY 37

While You Wait

But blessed is the one who trusts in the Lord,
      whose confidence is in him.
They will be like a tree planted by the water
      that sends out its roots by the stream.
It does not fear when heat comes;
      its leaves are always green.
It has no worries in a year of drought
      and never fails to bear fruit. (Jeremiah 17:7–8)

Be still before the Lord; wait patiently for Him and entrust yourself to Him. (Psalm 37:7 AMP)

• •

May you walk by faith and not by sight when you're in an in-between space.

That place between promise and fulfillment, that gap between where you are and where you long to be.

That season of

not-yets,
what-ifs,
unanswered prayers,
circumstances beyond your control,
broken relationships,
loneliness,
weariness.

In this wilderness of waiting, may you yet dare to hope in him. Even in unexpected places, know that God is tenderly present.

Even if there aren't changes in your circumstances yet, changes are being made in you.

May this season of waiting be where you exchange your dependence on your surroundings and people for relying on Christ. May God's hidden, inner work in this time purify and refine you, set you free and release you from bondage and fear, and draw your eyes to the One closer than your very breath.

Even here, may you renew yourself in the refreshment of his presence, in the deep springs of his unfailing love.

The waiting may be just where God allows your roots to grow deep.

God, even in my season of wilderness and of waiting, may I experience your goodness, your presence, and your overflowing kindness to me.

DAY 38

An Extravagant Father

As a father has compassion on his children,
    so the LORD has compassion on those who fear him.
      (Psalm 103:13)

Trust that your heavenly Father longs to give you good things.

However life has influenced your idea of God as *Father*, may you know that your heavenly Father never withholds love or good gifts from his children.

Neither distant nor unkind, disinterested nor stingy, God is wholehearted in his affection—God doesn't like to punish but desires to bless!

Today he offers you his immense love and compassion—all of himself—without limit.

Believe he wants to give you the deepest desires of your heart.

Father, help me trust that you are a kind, affectionate Father moved to act on my behalf. Heal those inner places where my experiences have obscured the reality of your loving faithfulness and care.

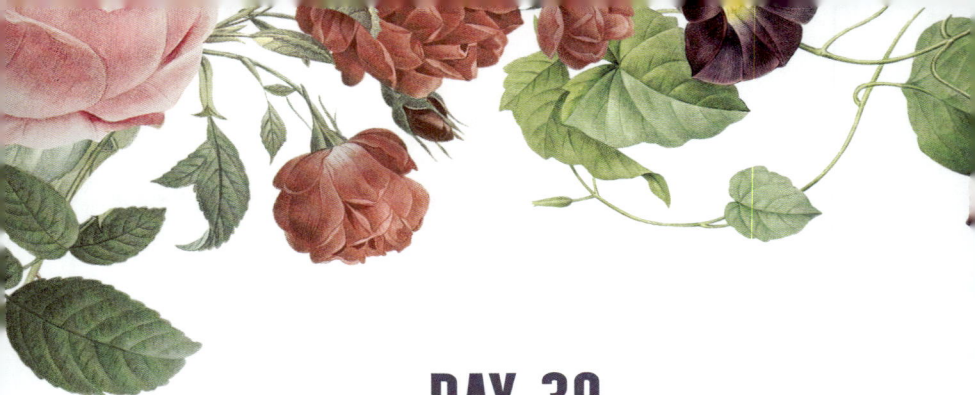

DAY 39

The Safety of Letting Go

Shortly before dawn Jesus went out to [the disciples], walking on the lake.

"Lord, if it's you," Peter replied, "tell me to come to you on the water."

"Come," [Jesus] said. Then Peter got down out of the boat, walked on the water and came toward Jesus. (Matthew 14:25, 28–29)

• •

May you risk going to the edge of your comfort when Jesus calls you near.

No matter what fears, anxieties, or regrets paralyze you from taking hold of all that God has for you, you can still listen to Jesus's gentle invitation:

Come.

Dare to lock eyes with Christ and hold your Savior's gaze.

God longs to take you by the hand—to guide you through this day, and all of its challenges and complexities.

Risk letting go.

In relinquishment and yielded trust, receive true fulfillment and safety.

But God will not force you to get out of the boat.

Will you listen to his beckoning voice?

Will you dare to walk on water?

Jesus, in your presence, I find the freedom and peace I long for. Empower me with trust and courage to let go of whatever is stopping me from taking hold of your hand and coming to you.

DAY 40

Finding Refuge in God

From the end of the earth I will cry to You,
When my heart is overwhelmed;
Lead me to the rock that is higher than I.
  (Psalm 61:2 NKJV)

May your heart find assurance and deep joy in God.

When your heart is overwhelmed and flooded with anxiety, may you know where to immediately turn.

Give yourself fully to the safety of God's eternal refuge.

In Christ, rest deeply.

While you're in his presence, may God soothe your fears, comfort you in the sanctuary of his love, and refresh your peace.

You are shielded on all sides by God's tremendous power.

With God, you are completely safe.

With God, your heart will be renewed.

With God, you will live valiantly.

Quiet yourself in him.

Father, when I cry out, I know you hear me. Keep your eye on me and comfort me, strengthen me, and sustain me. You are my refuge and strong tower.

DAY 41

Trusting His Love

Let us then approach God's throne of grace with confidence, so that we may receive mercy and find grace to help us in our time of need. (Hebrews 4:16)

. . . .

Whatever your failures, fears, or disappointments, may you trust—above all else—that God invites you to approach his throne with confidence.

In your hour of trial, in your failures, in your need, he promises to receive you without judgment. Christ will never reject you, refuse you, or turn you away.

God loves you without reservation, without hesitation.

May you know that his love for you won't change, no matter what.

Trust that, whatever your circumstances, disappointments, or challenges, his arms are wide open in invitation.

You are loved with an everlasting love.

God, give me the confidence and faith that whatever my circumstances or choices, you offer unconditional, eternal love for me. Help me to receive your love with vulnerability and trust.

DAY 42

Free and Forgiven

Therefore, there is now no condemnation for those who are in Christ Jesus. (Romans 8:1)

May you know how completely you are forgiven and how deeply you are loved.

No matter your past mistakes, your current struggles, or your future failures, may you refuse to believe that condemnation is yours.

May you instead tune in to God's love song for you: you are wholly redeemed, immensely cherished, and uniquely appointed.

You are his child: his daughter, honored in his sight, and powerful in Christ.

So, take hold of his promises. Trust in his grace. Embrace your identity in him.

God, thank you for the amazing gifts of your forgiveness and love. Help me embrace the freedom and restoration you offer in the areas where I still experience shame or condemnation. I love you!

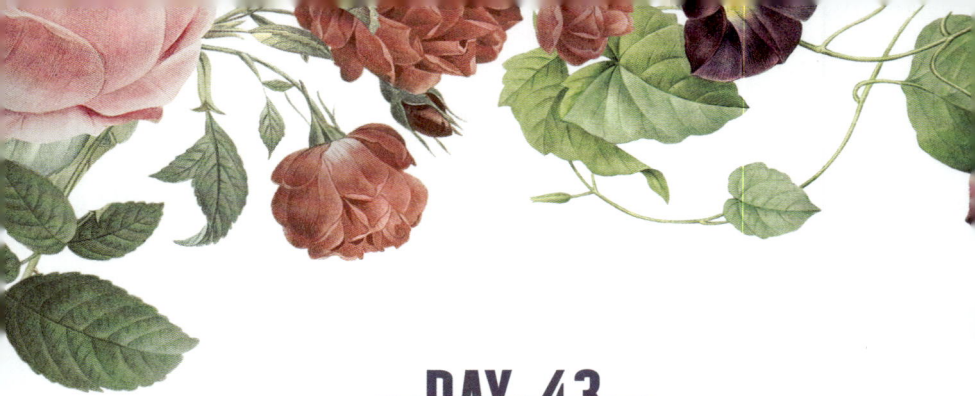

DAY 43

When You Need Forgiveness

For as high as the heavens are above the earth,
   so great is his love for those who fear him;
as far as the east is from the west,
   so far has he removed our transgressions from us.
      (Psalm 103:11–12)

I will . . . remember their sins no more. (Hebrews 8:12)

May regrets that have piled up over the years be fully released to God.

No matter your mistakes, he has removed them as far as the east is from the west. God has completely wiped them away.

You are not who you once were—you have been remade, being transformed each day by his grace.

Whatever sins are in your past, God remembers them no more.

May you awaken to the reality that God is creating something new, alive—beautiful—in you. You are his beloved child, divinely chosen, unequivocally redeemed, and he is calling you to step out and walk confidently in this fresh new path.

Look up!

Dare to welcome the accepting, gracious way your heavenly Father sees you.

God, I have so many regrets for things I've done and left undone. Help me to see myself how you view me: as someone you love without qualification.

DAY 44

Bring What You Have

B ring them here to me," [Jesus] said. (Matthew 14:18)

He brought me out into a spacious place;
  he rescued me because he delighted in me.
    (Psalm 18:19)

. . . .

May you feel God's deep joy as you dare to be yourself with him.

When you pray, bring what you have:

the beautiful, the raw, the vulnerable, the hard, the unfinished, the unpolished, the fragmented.

Risk coming before him honestly: to rage and rejoice, to laugh and lament, to cry and to shout aloud.

Experience God's delight as you try something new, steadfastly stick with a task, or entrust your deepest desires, goals, and concerns to him.

Inhale. Exhale. Enter God's presence with the relaxed confidence that—whatever your hardships or heartaches—you are buoyed and upheld by the One who loves you perfectly, who sees you through the eyes of immense grace and compassion, and who has committed himself to you for eternity.

May you show up each and every day alive to God and present to yourself.

God, what an amazing freedom I have to come before you, the King of Kings, with my honest thoughts, feelings, and concerns. May I delight in you as you delight in me.

DAY 45

Ask and Receive

For everyone who asks, receives. Everyone who seeks, finds. And to everyone who knocks, the door will be opened. (Matthew 7:8 NLT)

God sees your faithfulness, he is proud of your courage, and he hears your prayers.

May you not give up hoping, expecting—waiting for him to do what you cannot do on your own.

May you press in when the harvest seems far off.

May you trust that above all else, God is merciful and God of the miraculous.

Don't be surprised when he answers your prayers.

Ask and you shall receive.

Jesus, you are a God of miracles. May I yield to your wisdom and ways as I wait on you, your breakthroughs, and your limitless provision.

DAY 46

The Lord Who Heals
(*Yahweh Rophe*)

I am the LORD, who heals you. (Exodus 15:26)

A woman was there who had been subject to bleeding for twelve years. . . . When she heard about Jesus, she came up behind him in the crowd and touched his cloak.

He said to her, "Daughter, your faith has healed you. Go in peace and be freed from your suffering." (Mark 5:25, 27, 34)

. . . .

THE LORD WHO HEALS (*Yahweh Rophe*). The Hebrew term *rophe* means "cure," "repair," "heal," or "make whole." It encompasses not just physical healing but healing of mind and soul. In the Old Testament, God heals diseases, restores the brokenhearted, and saves and delivers those bound by sin (Psalm 103:3; 107:17–20; 147:3). In the New Testament, we see Jesus healing the blind, curing diseases, forgiving sins, and even giving life back to those who had died (Matthew 9:1–8; Mark 2:1–12; John 9; 11).

. . . .

When you have unanswered prayers and unmet needs, may you refuse to give up. May you—in prayer—dare to press in and continually enter God's presence.

May you risk taking hold of the Great Healer's cloak, trusting that his intentions are good, and that he would never willingly withhold his best gifts from his children.

May you have faith to believe that—in his timing, in his purposes, and in his ways—you will receive fresh hope and wholeness again.

God delights in your bold trust, and he is pleased with your ways. Believe that he who is in the business of healing deeply desires to bring about renewal and revival in your life.

Know that you can trust him.

Yahweh Rophe, when I'm seeking healing and wholeness, help me to go boldly before you, trusting that you care for me and that you long to bring about my restoration and full health.

DAY 47

A Meal with God

I will be fully satisfied as with the richest of foods;
>   with singing lips my mouth will praise you.
>   (Psalm 63:5)

Open your mouth and taste, open your eyes and see—
    how good God is.
Blessed are you who run to him. (Psalm 34:8 MSG)

Come, all you who are thirsty,
    come to the waters;
and you who have no money,
    come, buy and eat!
Come, buy wine and milk
    without money and without cost. . . .
Listen, listen to me, and eat what is good,
    and you will delight in the richest of fare. (Isaiah 55:1–2)

. . . .

He's been waiting for you, longing to offer you his bounty.

May you sit down at his table—allow him to serve you.

He desires to give you the nourishment your heart and soul really need: the abundance of his provision, the aroma of his peace, the depths of his wisdom.

He's overjoyed for you to delight in the richest of fare.

Come, eat—stay awhile.

May you leave satisfied—completely content, perfectly at peace, and totally satiated—in him.

Jesus, thank you for the feast of your wisdom, strength, and encouragement. As I savor your provision, may I be wholly satisfied in you.

DAY 48

God of Goodness

Taste and see that the LORD is good;
    blessed is the one who takes refuge in him.
    (Psalm 34:8)

. . . .

May you taste and see that he is good.

You have a Savior who loves you, who likes you, who—in fact—delights in you.

He longs to hear your voice. He is attuned to your ways. He anticipates your every thought.

You are his beloved, the apple of his eye, and the jewel in his crown. You move the heart of the King of heaven and earth.

May you rest in the knowledge that he is gentle, humble, and kind. He will never force or coerce—he only invites and beckons.

Whatever your experience of imperfect, conditional love from your past or present, discover that his affection is completely safe.

May his love—a perfect love—drive out all your fear.

God, thank you for your perfect, unfailing love. Help me believe on a whole new level that I can trust you with everything.

DAY 49

For the Spaces Between

So do not fear, for I am with you;
   do not be dismayed, for I am your God.
I will strengthen you and help you;
   I will uphold you with my righteous right hand.
      (Isaiah 41:10)

· ·

When you're in an in-between space—not yet having arrived at your destination, but vowing not to go back the way you came—

may you experience your Father's unfailing grace.

He is with you there—in the uncertainty, discomfort, and yearning

as you dare to hope for something new

yet still feel paralyzed by the unknown.

Let him love you in all your doubts and indecision.

Allow him to sit with you—quietly. Similar to how a friend would—relaxed, unhurried—on a perfect summer evening. Christ is not interested in rushing you.

May the presence of Christ offer you the safety and freedom to take the next step

into your new beginning.

Jesus, thank you for giving me the courage to dare to hope for something new and for the peace of your constant presence with me, even when I hesitate to step forward into the unknown.

DAY 50

Take on a New Name

You shall be called by a new name
       that the mouth of the LORD will give.
You shall be a beautiful crown in the hand of the LORD
       and a royal diadem in the hand of your God.
You shall no more be termed Forsaken,
       and your land shall no more be termed Desolate;
but you shall be called My Delight Is in Her.
    (Isaiah 62:2–4 NRSVUE)

May the stigmas and shackles from names you've accumulated over the years be broken.

Whatever they are—whether *Unlovable, Forgotten, Unworthy*—and however long they have held you bound, may their ability to diminish you, break you, or make you feel small be unloosed.

God is doing something fresh and new! Your heavenly Father wants to drape you in the exquisite, luxurious names that are yours in Christ . . .

You are *Enough. Beloved. My Delight Is in Her.*

May you clothe yourself in the exalted names that will restore you to who you truly are, and who you are to God.

May you wear them with bold confidence and walk in them with refreshed vitality grounded in your life in him.

Dare to allow God to extravagantly clothe you in your authentic, radiant, glorious identity.

Jesus, embolden me to take on the names that are the emblem of my true identity in you. May you bring fresh healing through them and may they release me to walk unhindered, upright, and unashamed.

DAY 51

For Reclaiming What Was Broken

You intended to harm me, but God intended it for good to accomplish what is now being done, the saving of many lives. (Genesis 50:20)

And we know that in all things God works for the good of those who love him, who have been called according to his purpose. (Romans 8:28)

May what the enemy meant to break or destroy be remade and repurposed for your highest good.

God sees . . .

The way you have suffered.

The tears you have wept.

The betrayal that blindsided you.

Know this: God suffered and wept with you. Familiar with grief, your Savior was despised, rejected, a man of sorrows;

Christ willingly enters into your pain, and he tenderly holds and heals those who are heartbroken and hurting.

May Christ take what is broken and shattered and reshape it, weld it together, and recreate it.

No matter how it seems, God is reviving the fractured, damaged parts of your life into something luminous and beautiful.

Restorer and Healer, may you renew what the enemy sought to destroy, and revive the sparks of what may have seemed extinguished.

DAY 52

When You Face Trials

Let us run with perseverance the race marked out for us, fixing our eyes on Jesus, the pioneer and perfecter of faith. For the joy set before him he endured the cross, scorning its shame, and sat down at the right hand of the throne of God. (Hebrews 12:1–2)

We are hard pressed on every side, but not crushed; perplexed, but not in despair; persecuted, but not abandoned; struck down, but not destroyed. (2 Corinthians 4:8–9)

May you dare to press in for the joy awaiting you, no matter the cost.

May you throw off anything that hinders you from fixing your eyes on Christ, who is worthy to receive all glory, honor, and wisdom.

God assures you that, while you will experience setbacks and unexpected seasons, you will never be alone.

You may be discouraged, but, by his power, emboldened;

oppressed, but not overthrown;

confused, yet upheld by God's sustaining hope.

Take courage. Don't lose heart.

You will get up again.

Though you are promised trials and afflictions in this life, God assures you that he will give you the immense strength, power, and provision to run your race to its end.

Trust him.

Jesus, in these days of challenges and heartache, may I lift my eyes and run the race marked before me, following in your footsteps. Give me the courage and determination to go the distance.

DAY 53

Vulnerability in God's Presence

The eternal God is your dwelling place, and underneath are the everlasting arms. (Deuteronomy 33:27 ESV)

Dare to come before God with bold expectation and fresh anticipation.

In his presence, may you overcome your inner fears, frustrations, and the barriers preventing you from approaching him with vulnerability and confident trust.

May you know at the deepest part of yourself that you are loved just as you are. You are known and cherished.

In God, you are more than enough.

Risk trusting. The everlasting God is committed to you in a secure, unfailing, all-encompassing relationship of love.

Dare being completely seen by God.

Dare allowing him to shower you with deep affection and undivided attention.

Lift up your eyes, live boldly out of God's love for you, and feel the comforting joy of being eternally held in God's embrace.

God, thank you for the refreshing freedom and security of being seen and known in your presence. Help me receive your comforting assurance that you pursue me out of your love and limitless affection.

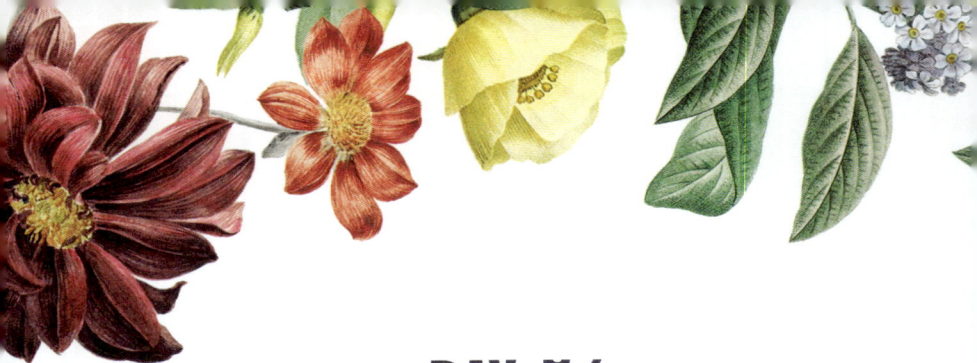

DAY 54

Homecoming

So [the prodigal son] returned home to his father. And while he was still a long way off, his father saw him coming. Filled with love and compassion, he ran to his son, embraced him, and kissed him. (Luke 15:20 NLT)

. . . .

Wherever you are on your journey—however far from home—know that you are never too distant to return to your heavenly Father.

God is already on his way to welcome you.

No matter your feelings of shame, no matter how far you've strayed, God will never reject you, ignore you, or turn you away.

Your heavenly Father loves you without reservation.

May his perfect love cast out all your fear.

May it liberate you to join in the heavenly homecoming party that he is throwing just for you.

God, may your perfect love for me cast out my fears. Thank you that—even with your knowledge of my shame and wandering—you always welcome me back home with mercy and compassion.

DAY 55

Embracing the New

Forget the former things;
    do not dwell on the past.
See, I am doing a new thing!
    Now it springs up; do you not perceive it?
I am making a way in the wilderness. (Isaiah 43:18–19)

Don't get so attached to old, familiar ways that you neglect to see his gifts in the present. God has operated faithfully before, but you have no idea how he's planning to bless you now.

Lean in—pay attention! He is doing a new thing!

Listen to the fresh revelation and renewal he is speaking over your life. Don't cling to the comforts of the past if God is in the process of doing something new.

You don't want to miss his fresh invitation—of peace and new life in him.

God, help me not to get so fixated on the past that I fail to pay attention to your present invitation. May I not underestimate how you accomplish your purposes in and through me in this season of my life.

DAY 56

Stay Hungry

For forty years I led you through the wilderness, yet your clothes and sandals did not wear out. (Deuteronomy 29:5 NLT)

· ·

When the promised land is beyond your line of sight, may you rise up in faith and determine to cling to God and his ways.

May you stay hungry for the things of God—

seek him and his Word—

and refuse to compromise, no matter the pressures from peers or the prevailing culture.

May you keep your eyes and heart transfixed on your Great Provider:

God offers you heavenly manna—daily protection, provision, and care—even when the promised land is outside your line of sight.

God will and is willing to fulfill his every promise to you, in his time and in his ways.

He is faithful. Hold on.

God, even in wilderness seasons, give me eyes to recognize your daily guidance, provision, and care. May I trust in you even when my journey is unexpected.

DAY 57

For Life in the Valley

The LORD is my shepherd. . . .
    Even when I walk
        through the darkest valley,
I will not be afraid,
        for you are close beside me.
Your rod and your staff
        protect and comfort me. (Psalm 23:1, 4 NLT)

I am the good shepherd. The good shepherd lays down his life for the sheep. (John 10:11)

You are weary. It's been a long day, a discouraging week, a soul-tiring journey.

May you trust that you aren't alone in this valley. That God sees your way, and your Good Shepherd hasn't abandoned you to navigate its pitfalls and snares without his guidance and protection.

May you experience his everlasting love in your afflictions.

May you sleep quietly tonight knowing that God shields you on all sides, has gated you in with his love, and will not allow you to fall prey to the enemy.

Christ's staff and shield are ready, and he is always on guard.

His love for you is unshakable, and you are precious to God.

God, thank you that you are the Good Shepherd. In both my waking and sleeping, I ask that you protect and lead, comfort and shelter me with your nurturing care.

DAY 58

When You Need Faith

I will answer them before they even call to me.
    While they are still talking about their needs,
    I will go ahead and answer their prayers!
        (Isaiah 65:24 NLT)

· ·

Blessed are you when you give the reality of your situation—your challenges, discouragement, and failures—to God.

May you see God come through in unexpected and miraculous ways. May you lift up your head with fresh hope and courageous expectation, worshiping the God who is faithful, worthy, and a worker of miracles.

Know this: God is not finished with this situation, or with you.

God is bringing about a harvest in his kingdom and in your life, and it is advancing—even if, at the moment, it is unseen.

Remember: you walk by faith, not by sight.

Jesus, give me fresh courage and new eyes
to trust that you are for me and with me,
and that nothing is too challenging for you.
Please make a way where there is no way.

DAY 59

When You Pray for Your Loved Ones

The prayer of a righteous person is powerful and effective. (James 5:16)

May you intercede on behalf of your loved ones with perseverance, faith, and confidence, knowing that God answers you.

May you trust that your prayers have great power and ignite a firestorm in the heavenly realms.

As you pray, may you see lives change, hearts awakened, and hope renewed. God is mighty to heal, sustain, uphold, and carry your loved ones through every trial and fear—he can do all things, in his timing, in his ways, and for his purposes!

May you trust God's process.

Father, help me to confidently and faithfully pray for my loved ones. May you strengthen their character, bring about renewal and healing, and encourage them in ways that only you can!

DAY 60

Resting in Abba God

Even to your old age I am He,
And even to your advanced old age I will carry you!
I have made you, and I will carry you;
Be assured I will carry you and I will save you.
  (Isaiah 46:4 AMP)

I have cared for you since you were born.
  Yes, I carried you before you were born.
I will be your God throughout your lifetime.
  (Isaiah 46:3–4 NLT)

You are held by the everlasting God.

Forever, you are protected, sustained, and accepted by Abba God.

Forever, you are hidden with Christ in God.

While you were yet in the womb, God gathered you in his strong arms and sang joyously over you. Every day since that day, God has carried and upheld you, sustained and reassured you, quietly consoled and comforted you.

May God lift you up and soothe you with the sweetness of his love.

Abba, you carried me before I was born, and you have promised to be my God throughout my lifetime. I trust in you.

DAY 61

Who You Are

Therefore, if anyone is in Christ, the new creation has come: The old has gone, the new is here! (2 Corinthians 5:17)

· ·

May you—in the depths of your being—ground yourself in the assurance and knowledge of *who* you are and *whose* you are:

> The Lord's beloved, child of God, royalty—seated with Christ in the heavenly realms;
>
> a friend of God, Jesus's coworker,
> a minister of reconciliation,
> a priest in Christ's kingdom;
>
> God's masterpiece, a radiant, new creation.

May you live out of the freedom of finding your identity in Christ.

God, whatever is keeping me from you—whether shame or self-condemnation—I ask that you enable me to receive your love in full measure.

DAY 62

The Lord Is My Banner
(*Yahweh Nissi*)

Moses built an altar and called it The Lᴏʀᴅ is my Banner. (Exodus 17:15)

May we shout for joy over your victory
   and lift up our banners in the name of our God.
      (Psalm 20:5)

· ·

THE LORD MY BANNER (*Yahweh Nissi*). Moses ascribed to God the name The Lord My Banner following God's miraculous deliverance of Israel over their enemy (Exodus 17:15–16). During war, ancient militia carried a banner representing a nation's identity, around which the army could appeal for power and protection.

Ann Spangler writes, "When you pray to *Yahweh Nissi*, you are praying to the God who is powerful enough to overcome any foe."*

· ·

On the day of your trial, may "*Yahweh Nissi*, the Lord Is My Banner" be your war cry.

---

*Ann Spangler, *Praying the Names of God for 52 Weeks: A Year-Long Bible Study*, exp. ed. (Grand Rapids, MI: HarperChristian Resources, 2023), 50.

Whenever the enemy accuses you of failings, fears, and past mistakes, may you refuse to listen to his taunts. Condemnation is not yours.

Under the banner of God's love, you are chosen, forgiven—free.

May you lift up your praise to God as a weapon of warfare, declaring that God is your healing victory. You are redeemed—liberated—found in him.

May he who overcame overthrow each lie of your enemy.

May *Yahweh Nissi* do battle on your behalf. He will do what you cannot do on your own.

Yahweh Nissi, *today I declare that my identity is found under the protective covering of your banner. When the accuser brings charges against me, help me appeal to the banner of your love, power, and overflowing mercy.*

DAY 63

The Battle Is Not Yours

This is what the LORD says to you: "Do not be afraid or discouraged because of this vast army. For the battle is not yours, but God's." (2 Chronicles 20:15)

Blessed are you when you give up fighting in your own strength.

The battle is not yours, but God's.

Instead, may you boldly embrace your role in combat:

show up armed—clothed in his divine armor;

reliant on his strength and power,

being prayerful, watchful—ready.

May you release your loved ones, your impossible situation, your unanswered prayers to God, allowing him to make your way straight.

Watch God march before you, on your behalf.

God, this battle is not mine but yours. Nothing is impossible with you, so I give you my loved ones, my impossible situation, my unmet expectations and ask you to do what I can't.

DAY 64

The Edge of Your Possible

Jesus looked at them and said, "With man this is impossible, but with God all things are possible." (Matthew 19:26)

. . . .

Blessed are you who've come to the edge of your possible.

Blessed are you who've experienced setbacks, failures, and discouragement, you who've pressed in and lost ground.

In these disorienting, unexpected, discouraging places, give yourself permission to fall headlong on the One who sees you with the eyes of tender love and boundless mercy.

Come, he calls to you. God promises that his yoke is easy and his burden is light.

Whatever your situation, you are not alone. Your loving Savior guarantees that his presence is yours, and he offers

you his strength and assurances of eternal hope. No matter your circumstances, the King of Kings is still in control and sovereign over the universe.

May he be your Guide, Comforter, and Protector as you navigate your way through your dark night.

In him, all things are possible.

Christ, I ask for the courage to walk by faith and not by sight. You are for me, with me, and will never leave me or forsake me. Please guide, direct, and protect me today.

DAY 65

He Will Make a Way

Moses answered the people, "Do not be afraid. Stand firm and you will see the deliverance the LORD will bring you today. The Egyptians you see today you will never see again. The LORD will fight for you; you need only to be still." (Exodus 14:13–14)

. . . .

May you cling to God, whatever your circumstances. Today, may you make a vow: you are committed to him, whatever the cost.

When aligned with his purposes, timing, and will, you don't have to be anxious. Be still.

Be expectant. On all sides are your Red Sea impossibilities; wait deliberately for his deliverance. When yielded to God, you don't have to be afraid.

No longer immobilized by fear, watch as Jesus opens up the path before you, sweeping the waters of adversity,

ambiguity, and oppression aside to establish your path on dry ground.

God will make a way where there is no way.

He will fight for you. Be still.

God, even when I cannot see the path, I give my circumstances to you, trusting that you will move mightily on my behalf. Thank you for making a way for me.

DAY 66

Wisdom in the Waiting

May he grant you your heart's desire
    and fulfill all your plans! (Psalm 20:4 ESV)

In this instant gratification culture, may you have the wisdom and fortitude to wait on God.

May you discern between temporary distractions and what satisfies the deepest longings of your heart.

May you dare to seek your heart's desires openly and honestly, no matter how it appears.

May you have fresh expectancy and renewed anticipation that God desires to answer your prayers and fulfill your deepest longings.

Wait on God with confidence and conviction. He is faithful and will renew your strength.

God, discouragement and disappointments often lead me to question you and your ways. Whatever my circumstances, help me to wait on and trust in you and believe that you have good plans and purposes for my family and for me.

DAY 67

He Is with You

The LORD is the one who is going ahead of you; He will be with you. He will not desert you or abandon you. Do not fear and do not be dismayed. (Deuteronomy 31:8 NASB)

. . . .

May you allow God to tenderly lead you through this day.

Go gently

or tackle that problem headlong—

knowing that neither is right nor wrong when done in trusting dependence on him.

May you have confidence that for every situation, Christ will give what is needed—sufficient grace, wisdom, and abundant provision—to show up, to be present . . .

to love and be loved,

to give and receive,

to live God's kingdom on earth.

So, quiet yourself. Pause. Listen.

In all your activities, in both the momentous and mundane, may you rely on him—experiencing the joy of collaborating with the King of Kings. In your every moment, in every decision—

may you trust him in all things.

Jesus, you promise to provide me with strength for today. Thank you for partnering with me in my responsibilities and collaborating with me in my tasks and challenges, no matter how big or small they are.

DAY 68

An Invitation to Notice

The purposes of a person's heart are deep waters,
but one who has insight draws them out.
(Proverbs 20:5)

. . . .

Today, may you notice when you feel worthy—
and when you feel guilt or shame.

May you pay attention to what is life-giving—
and when your energy and strength are completely drained.

May you recognize when you experience safety and love—
and when you feel paralyzed by fear.

May you tune in to when you feel close to God—
and when you feel distant or unable to hear from him.

May you listen and discern God's still, small voice, whatever
the background noise.

No matter the movements of your heart today, may you know that God is steadfastly with you all the same. But the more you can *notice, pay attention*, and *listen* to the fluctuations of your thoughts, feelings, and emotions, the more you can offer them to God and receive his fresh strength, deep peace, and life-sustaining healing.

God, today I commit to paying attention to my attitudes and actions. I release them to you and receive your comfort, support, and power.

DAY 69

Living Worthy

Just as He chose us in Him before the foundation of the world, that we should be holy and without blame before Him in love. (Ephesians 1:4 NKJV)

· ·

May you accept and love yourself as you are, knowing that Jesus has already accepted you and loves you wholeheartedly, with no strings attached.

May you exchange striving and perfectionism for receiving God's unconditional favor and openhearted affection. However you feel, you captivate and delight God and are infinitely precious to your Savior. You are his beloved.

May you speak words of life and freedom over yourself, because Jesus speaks words of hope and encouragement—not condemnation—over you.

May you relinquish your unknowns and place them into the all-knowing One's hands.

May you believe in yourself—out of the truth that, even before you were born—God dared to believe in you.

Jesus, free me from any lies that drive me to strive for approval and affection when I already possess your wholehearted acceptance and love.

DAY 70

Belonging to Abba God

Because we are his children, God has sent the Spirit of his Son into our hearts, prompting us to call out, "Abba, Father." (Galatians 4:6 NLT)

Amid the flurry of your tasks and responsibilities, may you take a second, pause—breathe.

Whisper to your soul, "I belong to Abba God." Let the assurance of this truth trickle into your mind and heart.

Then go about your day—

grounded in the knowledge that the God of the universe holds you firmly, securely, always.

You are Abba God's, now and forever.

Abba God, I belong to you. Wherever I go today, help me know that I am enveloped by the comfort and surety of your calming, sheltering presence.

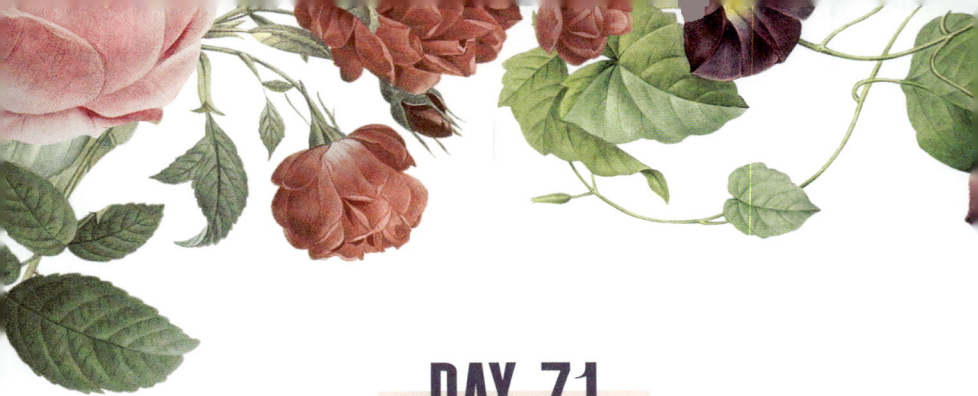

DAY 71

You're Not Being Asked to Save the World

M ary . . . sat at the Lord's feet listening to what he said. . . .

[Jesus commended Mary:] "Few things are needed—or indeed only one. Mary has chosen what is better, and it will not be taken away from her." (Luke 10:39, 42)

Don't worry: you're not being asked to save the world,

or to set aside your tasks,

or to pray big prayers.

For just a moment or two, let go of your never-ending to-do list, forget your agenda, and sit with Jesus.

Showing up is enough. (Jesus simply likes your company.)

May you feel safe, relaxed, and alive in Christ's presence. Here in this space, may Jesus reassure your heart, refresh your courage, and renew your trust in him.

Let yourself feel the wonder and joy of having God's undivided attention.

May your listening become a prayer.

May the Lord give you his comforting assurance that whatever you do the rest of your day, he goes with you.

Jesus, free me of the compulsion to strive or perform in your presence. Embolden me to accept your love and reassurance in vulnerability and trust. Help me to rest, relax, and freely enjoy your sweet company.

DAY 72

Where Mercy and Truth Meet

Mercy and truth have met together;
    Righteousness and peace have kissed.
    (Psalm 85:10 NKJV)

You can be loving and strong.

You can be on the side of mercy and truth.

You can say no.

You have the freedom to forgive.

You can choose the brave thing while still being afraid.

You can be kind yet set healthy boundaries.

You can do hard things.

You can honor grief and rejoice freely.

May the Holy Spirit guide you for how to lean in to the tension of embodying both righteousness and peace.

Holy Spirit, guide and direct me to choose wisely and live from a grounded space of strength, courage, and freedom. When you call me to stand up and speak, empower me to raise my voice; when you ask that I have self-restraint, I ask for the wisdom and self-control to listen.

DAY 73

Enough Already!

The LORD your God in your midst, . . .
He will rejoice over you with gladness,
He will quiet you with His love,
He will rejoice over you with singing.
(Zephaniah 3:17 NKJV)

. . . .

Enough already! For too long, you've tried too hard—tending to everyone's needs, trying to make them happy.

If only for a moment, allow God to attend to you with the same generous care you offer everyone else.

May God sing softly over you, his lullabies grounding and reminding you of who you are, and who you are to him.

May you allow God to gently carry and quietly console you.

No matter how childish it feels to be held, before your role as [caregiver, leader, daughter, sister, wife, mother, friend], you are first his beloved child.

In God's embrace, feel the comfort of knowing how deeply you are loved.

*Heavenly Father, thank you for calling me
to come to you in childlike faith and trust.
Help me enter the rest that comes from being
held in your strong, nurturing arms.*

DAY 74

Worship in the Waiting

There was also a prophet, Anna, the daughter of Penuel, of the tribe of Asher. She was very old; she had lived with her husband seven years after her marriage, and then was a widow until she was eighty-four. She never left the temple but worshiped night and day, fasting and praying. Coming up to them at that very moment, she gave thanks to God and spoke about the child to all who were looking forward to the redemption of Jerusalem. (Luke 2:36–38)

No matter the noise and chaos of surrounding culture, may you not forsake your fire and passion for God. Like the prophet Anna of old, may you live your life in heartfelt anticipation and renewed hope of the coming King.

May you seek his kingdom first and continually transfix your eyes on him.

May you press in to prayer and release yourself to praise.

Whatever your season or stage of life, may you—like the prophet—dare to take the prophet's mantle:

to give thanks to God

and attest to the peace, strength, and deep joy that he brings.

God, I'm easily distracted. In a world of confusion and constant chaos, help me to press in to the thing that really matters: seeking you and your ways. No matter what, I know that you are in control, that you will lead me through, and that you are in the process of making everything new.

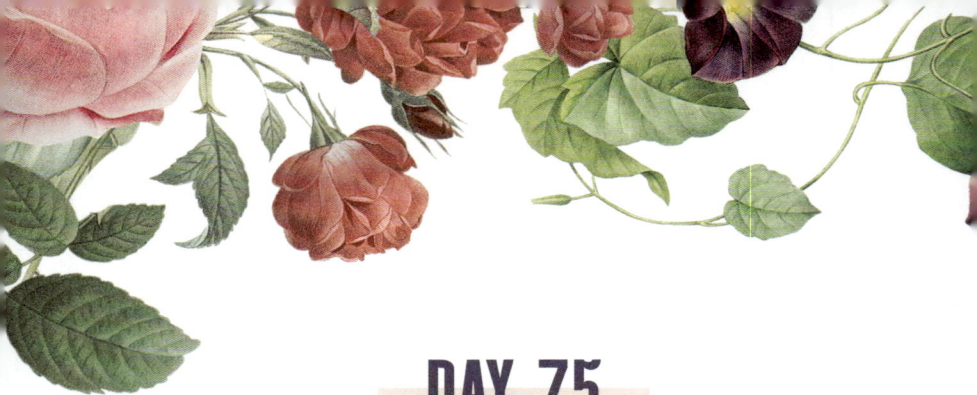

DAY 75

Lord (*Yahweh*)

Moses said to God, "Suppose I go to the Israelites and say to them, 'The God of your fathers has sent me to you,' and they ask me, 'What is his name?' Then what shall I tell them?"

God said to Moses, "I AM WHO I AM.* This is what you are to say to the Israelites: 'I AM [Yahweh] has sent me to you.'" (Exodus 3:13–14)

LORD (*Yahweh*). God revealed this personal, sacred name when he drew near to the Israelites in their distress, rescued them from bondage, and called them into a covenant relationship with himself (Exodus 3:13–15). Meaning "he is," or "he will be," the name *Yahweh* demonstrates that God is all-powerful: infinite, self-sufficient, self-existent, and everlasting.

In the context of God's deliverance and profession of love for his people, the name also hints at God's nearness: *Yahweh* is present, fiercely protective, eternally devoted, willing and able to respond to his people's needs, and desiring an intimate, exclusive relationship with those he loves.

---

*Or "I WILL BE WHAT I WILL BE."

May the eternal, infinite One, the Creator beyond time and space, meet you in your present moment.

Though infinite, he is also gentle and lowly.

Though unchanging, God is not unmoved by your courage, heartaches, and fears.

Though self-existent, God is not dispassionate or detached. He desires to bind himself to you forever in covenant love. Out of fervent devotion, God burns with passion and is fiercely jealous of your love for him.

He is the One who was, who is, and who is to come. He is the Alpha and Omega, the beginning and the end.

May you completely entrust yourself to the great I AM, who will be with you and for you, now and forever.

Yahweh, thank you that though you transcend time and space, you have drawn close to me in love. Thank you for desiring a deep, genuine relationship with me. Draw me ever closer to you.

DAY 76

Joyful Dependence on God

Why, you do not even know what will happen tomorrow. What is your life? You are a mist that appears for a little while and then vanishes. Instead, you ought to say, "If it is the Lord's will, we will live and do this or that." (James 4:14–15)

• •

Today, may you embrace being human:

Listen to your limits.

Dare to feel wild, unbridled joy.

Press in . . . or let go.

Ask for help.

Get rest.

Let God come close. You weren't meant to carry the burdens of this world alone. Whatever your uncertainties,

enthusiasms, or cares, may you freely release them into God's open hands and receive his vast comfort, encouragement, and immeasurable provision for your every need.

Your heavenly Father desires to embrace you in the breadth of your beauty, in the wildness of your emotions, in the fullness of your humanity.

Heavenly Father, today help me embrace my limits and release to you today's knowns and unknowns, my habits and decisions, my joys and my disappointments, trusting that you hold them all in the palms of your hands.

DAY 77

When You Feel Incomplete

I have learned the secret of living in every situation, whether it is with a full stomach or empty, with plenty or little. For I can do everything through Christ, who gives me strength. (Philippians 4:12–13 NLT)

May your soul-hunger and longings draw you closer to God.

Let your emptiness and the aches of this life cause you to fall freely in God's arms and compel you to seek his overflowing provision and power for your every need.

Don't deny, diminish, or set aside your feelings of brokenness and pain, but instead, offer and release them in God's presence.

Only when we release our heartaches can God fully heal them.

Only in acknowledging that we are incomplete can we completely accept the tenderness, help, and abundant wisdom Jesus longs to give so freely.

May you offer your weaknesses, dreams and desires, and uncertainties and receive the God of all comfort's reassuring strength, guidance, and encouragement each day.

May you sit quietly at his feet.

God is safe, gentle, and kind. Hide yourself in God's eternal protection and profound peace.

In God's presence, release and receive.

God of all comfort, help me release my pain, heartaches, and insecurities and receive your inordinate strength, courage, and power to face each day's trials and circumstances. Let my longings and need draw me ever closer to you.

DAY 78

The Promise of Heaven

And after you have suffered a little while, the God of all grace, who has called you to his eternal glory in Christ, will himself restore, confirm, strengthen, and establish you. (1 Peter 5:10 ESV)

. . . .

May your hope of heaven give you the courage to press on in the here and now.

Whatever your unexpected circumstances or challenges in this life, may you face your unknowns and overcome every fear protected by an eternal perspective.

Despite living in a world of not-yets, what-ifs, and in-betweens, may you lift up your eyes and seek this life-changing truth:

You were not designed for this world. You're just passing through. Let that release you from the pressure of seeking ultimate fulfillment or eternal satisfaction from anyone or anything in the here and now.

Dare to embrace life with abandon and without fear.

You have an unshakable promise of heaven and an eternal hope awaiting you. Let that truth empower you to lean in to the always open, always welcoming arms of your heavenly Father, who promises to give you everything you need and to present you with an unshakable, abundant inheritance for all eternity.

In the meantime, may the hope of heaven liberate you to let go of the small things.

And may it free you to take joy in the small things too.

Jesus, help me daily remember that I am promised an eternity with you so that I can confidently run this race and freely enjoy your good gifts.

DAY 79

The Wonder of the Small

Do not despise these small beginnings, for the LORD rejoices to see the work begin. (Zechariah 4:10 NLT)

Rejoice! No matter how insignificant or small it may seem, this is a day of new beginnings.

May you celebrate these small beginnings, because God celebrates them with the same enthusiasm as he does their completion and conclusion.

May you cut off all that discourages you from pressing in to the end.

Take hold of what lies ahead.

May you find joy in the breakthrough, peace amidst opposition, and fresh courage to quiet every fear.

Whatever your journey, you can trust that you are assured of a good ending.

Take heart: God won't let you fail.

God, thank you for new beginnings, fresh starts, and revived faith. Help me to press in and have perseverance to run the race to its end.

DAY 80

King of Kings (*Basileus Basileon*)

On his robe and on his thigh he has this name written:
KING OF KINGS AND LORD OF LORDS.
(Revelation 19:16)

Look at the birds of the air; they do not sow or reap or store away in barns, and yet your heavenly Father feeds them. Are you not much more valuable than they? Can any one of you by worrying add a single hour to your life? . . .

But seek first his kingdom and his righteousness, and all these things will be given to you as well. (Matthew 6:26–27, 33)

• •

KING OF KINGS (*Basileus Basileon*). Although Christ first appeared on earth as a humble baby, during his second return, Jesus will be welcomed as the King of Kings (Revelation 19:16), the majestic, sovereign, and victorious ruler of the visible and unseen world. While transcendent, the King of Kings also draws near to us. In Matthew 6:33, Jesus makes this promise to all who seek first the King of Kings and his kingdom: *everything* you need will be given to you.

• •

May you release your cares to God, knowing that he cares for you.

May you let go of the burdens and anxieties you cannot carry:
    The things in the past you cannot change.
    The things in the present you cannot control.
    The things in the future beyond your understanding.

God desires to take care of your every need.

May you exchange worries about the past, present, and future for your first concern: to seek the king and his wisdom.*

Entrust yourself to the God who tenderly clothes the lilies of the field and attentively watches over the life of every sparrow.

King of Kings, I'm in awe and wonder of your power and love. You reign and rule over the cosmos and the seen and unseen world, yet you also promise to care and provide for my every need.

---

*Adapted from Gary Inrig, *The Parables: Understanding What Jesus Meant* (Grand Rapids, MI: Discovery House Publishers, 1991), 105.

DAY 81

Your Exalted Position

And God . . . seated us with him in the heavenly realms in Christ Jesus. (Ephesians 2:6)

May you no longer stoop with condemnation or shame—

but rise in exultation to the One who is king of heaven and earth.

Do you know your exalted position in heaven? That even now, at all times, you sit next to Christ in the throne room, basking in his glory, power, and love?

From this seated position—a place of rest—you can stand,

walk,

run the race.

You don't have to earn or fight for his approval and acceptance—it's already yours.

What a privileged and glorious inheritance you possess!

Jesus, thank you that I do not have to strive for or earn your acceptance or approval. Help me live out of the security of having entered into your rest for me.

DAY 82

Holding Tightly

For if we are faithful to the end, trusting God just as firmly as when we first believed, we will share in all that belongs to Christ. (Hebrews 3:14 NLT)

• •

May you hold tightly to God, knowing that he holds you close in an ever-changing world.

May you loosen your grip on external, temporary things and open your hands to receive the eternal, unbreakable inheritance that is already yours.

Beloved, did you know that you are wealthy beyond your wildest dreams? Your heavenly Father has gifted you with every spiritual blessing in the heavenly realms!

Reflect on that truth with gratitude.

Whatever your current reality, your Abba God does not withhold or begrudge you anything but gives radically and lavishly to his children.

Abba God, it's hard to fathom the vast treasures that you have stored up for me. Thank you for blessing me with generous gifts. Help me trust confidently in you for all things.

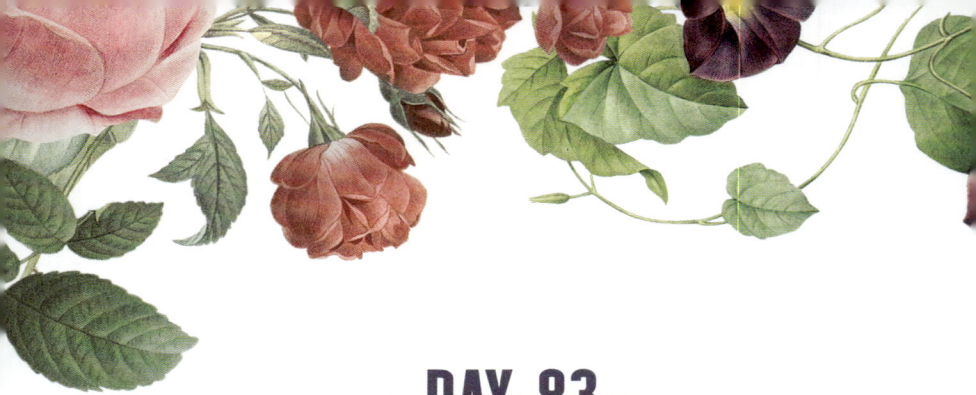

DAY 83

Declaring Victory

The Lord GOD is my strength [my source of courage, my
      invincible army];
He has made my feet [steady and sure] like hinds' feet
And makes me walk [forward with spiritual confidence]
      on my high places [of challenge and responsibility].
      (Habakkuk 3:19 AMP)

In the area of your struggle, trial, or insecurity, may you
trust that God will secure your way—

that he will personally protect your steps.

Where you once stumbled, may you stand upright—free.

Where you once fled in fear, may you gain the higher
ground.

Where you once were defeated, may you tread on your high
places of struggle, declaring victory.

May you trust that in all things, he will make your way
straight.

Almighty God, you are my source of strength and courage. Make my feet steady and sure, and help me to stand and run on my places of discouragement and fear.

DAY 84

Safety in God

The LORD is good,
  a stronghold in the day of trouble;
he knows those who take refuge in him. (Nahum 1:7 ESV)

. . . .

Blessed are you who run to God.

May God lift you high when you feel insecure and unsafe.

May he hold you securely when you feel anxious and afraid.

May his strong arms comfort and protect you when you feel exposed, unworthy, and ashamed.

May his lasting reassurance and quiet protection soothe your mind and calm your soul.

God holds you closely.

Blessed are you who, in his arms, can't be moved.

God, in your presence, I am safe and unafraid
and able to live freely. Calm my heart and
my fears; allow me to rest deeply in you.

DAY 85

On God's Way

Jesus answered, "I am the way and the truth and the life." (John 14:6)

• •

When you feel like you've lost your way, remember that Jesus is the Way.

Stay close to him.

Where you experience inadequacy and need, remember that your Provider promises to give you bread for today.

Depend on him.

When you're anxious and afraid about your future, remember who created tomorrow.

Trust him.

When you don't have the eyes to see beyond today's confusion, remember that God holds the unseen.

Wait on him.

May you allow God to be
　　your Way,
　　your Provider,
　　your Wisdom.

Everything you need can be found in Christ.

Cast your cares on Jesus.

Jesus, in my circumstances and decisions today, may you be my Way, my Provider, my Wisdom. I ask that you guide me, protect me, carry me, and direct me through whatever this day may bring.

DAY 86

Waking Up to a Wartime Mentality

The weapons we fight with are not the weapons of the world. On the contrary, they have divine power to demolish strongholds. (2 Corinthians 10:4)

Always remember you are at war.

In these final days, may you exchange a peacetime mentality for a wartime posture.

At all times, stand armed:

A wartime mentality begins with simply attending to your physical and spiritual needs. Get rest. Eat healthily. Seek community. Give generously. Refresh yourself daily in God's presence. Tune out relentless distractions.

Above all, may you fix your mind on God and his perfect peace. God's peace that passes understanding will shield your mind and heart, enabling you to stand.

Even when you fail and fall, nothing—absolutely nothing—can keep you from landing in the embrace of God's limitless love.

Because Christ overcame, you are assured of total victory.

God, if I'm honest, I can feel sorry for myself when I face trials and struggles. Help me recognize that as a Christian, I'm not exempt from suffering, but I am engaged in spiritual war at all times. Equip me for this battle so I can advance your purposes and put my confidence in your ultimate victory.

DAY 87

God of the Breakthrough

This is what the LORD says— . . .
 "But forget all that—
   it is nothing compared to what I am going to do.
For I am about to do something new.
   See, I have already begun! Do you not see it?
I will make a pathway through the wilderness.
   I will create rivers in the dry wasteland."
    (Isaiah 43:14, 18–19 NLT)

May that which is barricaded in your life unlock.

May what is hidden be revealed.

May the Lord offer refreshment and life-giving healing for what has been shattered and broken in the past.

Ask him to awaken your courage: what God can do is beyond what you expect or fathom.

Is anything too hard for him?

God opens up what is walled off, relieves dry and weary hearts, and resurrects joy and peace in spirits filled with fear.

Jesus makes a way in the wilderness and streams in the desert.

The God of the breakthrough goes ahead of you.

God, enable me to look beyond my past so that I don't miss what you're doing now. Refresh my hope and revive my expectations that you are in the business of restoration and healing.

DAY 88

The Things We Carry

My yoke is easy and my burden is light. (Matthew 11:30)

What is it that you carry today?

Along your journey, you have collected things—

responsibilities,

burdens,

losses,

joys,

fears,

worries—like shells on the sand.

Over the years, some you intentionally selected; others were flung carelessly in your hand. A few have been stowed in your pocket many miles. Perhaps many years.

Are there any you can set aside?

Take time to hold them gently in your hands, inspect them, examine them, and discern whether to store or let go of them.

The truth is that some things God did not intend for you to keep a moment longer.

May you find the freedom to walk forward and release them.

Jesus, help me discern between what I'm called to carry and what I can relinquish. I ask for faithfulness to keep what is mine to steward, and the courage to let go of the things that are not mine to hold.

DAY 89

Earning or Receiving?

Do not be afraid, little flock, for your Father has been pleased to give you the kingdom. (Luke 12:32)

Be encouraged: a relationship with God is not about earning, but receiving.

It's not about striving, but about resting quietly in God's arms.

May you cease grasping and start releasing. Your God desires you to cast and release all your cares on him.

May you stop trying so hard and cease endlessly seeking God's approval.

Pause.

Relax, and let go.

Your heavenly Father is enthralled with you, calls you his child, has freely handed you his everlasting kingdom.

May you trade the illusion of control

for the freedom of fully surrendering to him.

God, you will never fail me. Help me to surrender and entrust myself to you, even when I'm scared to let go of control.

DAY 90

Prince of Peace (*Sar Shalom*)

For to us a child is born,
>to us a son is given,
>and the government will be on his shoulders.
And he will be called
>Wonderful Counselor, Mighty God,
>Everlasting Father, Prince of Peace. (Isaiah 9:6)

Do not be anxious about anything, but in every situation, by prayer and petition, with thanksgiving, present your requests to God. And the peace of God, which transcends all understanding, will guard your hearts and your minds in Christ Jesus. (Philippians 4:6–7)

PRINCE OF PEACE (*Sar Shalom*). In Hebrew, peace (*shalom*) means not only the absence of conflict but also having right relationships between ourselves and God, humanity, and all of creation. As the prophesied Prince of Peace, Jesus came to earth to restore our relationship with God and with each other (Isaiah 9:6).

When worry crowds your heart, may you hand your present concerns over to the God of all peace.

As you sit in God's gentle, powerful presence, may his peace become a seal of protection against your mind's persistent attacks of fear and anxiety.

May you experience fresh courage in your conflict, nourishing calm in your challenges, and reassuring hope in your adversity.

No matter the situation, the Prince of Peace is willing, desirous, and able to meet your every need, to care for your loved ones, and to do what is impossible for you to do on your own.

Let *Sar Shalom* wrap your soul in his perfect peace that passes all understanding.

Prince of Peace, let your perfect peace reign in my heart and my mind. I ask that you care for [situation, loved one, concern] and surround the situation with your protective love and lasting peace.

DAY 91

Going Home Another Way

The star they had seen when it rose went ahead of them until it stopped over the place where the child was. When they saw the star, they were overjoyed. On coming to the house, they saw the child with his mother Mary, and they bowed down and worshiped him. Then they opened their treasures and presented him with gifts of gold, frankincense and myrrh. And having been warned in a dream not to go back to Herod, they returned to their country by another route. (Matthew 2:9–12)

* *

When you cross a threshold of new beginnings,
may you know not to go plodding in the same direction, to
return by the way you came.

When you receive discernment and God's guidance,
let Jesus lead you safely through the danger, snares, and
pitfalls along your path.

When you are warned in a dream, vision, or prayer to go home another way,
may you trust the wisdom of God's infinite mercy and guidance.

Take courage.

Stand your ground.

Dare to listen to what the Spirit is whispering to you.

God, help me to heed the Spirit's warning and whispers in my life. When you give me knowledge of danger, temptations, or pitfalls along my journey, I pray that I would listen.

DAY 92

Unbroken Promise of Heaven

We don't look at the troubles we can see now; rather, we fix our gaze on things that cannot be seen. For the things we see now will soon be gone, but the things we cannot see will last forever. (2 Corinthians 4:18 NLT)

You weren't made for this world.

May you lift your eyes to the eternal, unbroken promise of heaven.

May you make ready your heart and mind for your everlasting home.

May you let go of misplaced hopes and take hold of your unshakable security: God cares for you; he will never leave you nor forsake you.

Trust him to provide for and protect you.

Your emptiness and soul hunger can only be fulfilled in him.

God, when I am discouraged, remind me that
on this earth, I am only passing through.
Nothing can provide me with ultimate
fulfillment and satisfaction in this life.
Strengthen my joy and contentment in you.

DAY 93

Sustained by Everlasting Love

I have loved you, my people, with an everlasting love.
With unfailing love I have drawn you to myself.
(Jeremiah 31:3 NLT)

. . . .

May God's steadfast love steady and reassure you.

May his calming assurance embolden you to dream and take risks.

In his presence, may you be released to strengthen and uplift, to overcome and expand territory, to take hold and triumph, to bravely persevere and boldly stand.

When you fail and fall, may you have the courage to come home to God.

Whatever your insecurities or mistakes, may God's acceptance and unfailing love draw you closer to himself.

Lift up your heart! Christ loves you with an everlasting, committed love.

Jesus, in your presence, I am healed, sustained, and strengthened to live out your eternal plans and purposes. May your everlasting love for me overcome my every fear.

Friend (*Philos*)

There is no greater love than to lay down one's life for one's friends. (John 15:13 NLT)

FRIEND (*Philos*). Astonishingly, Jesus calls all who follow him not just his subjects but his friends (John 15:12–15). The Greek word for friend—*philos*—is linked to a common Greek word for love, *phileo*. When speaking about friendship, Jesus said, "There is no greater love than to lay down one's life for one's friends" (John 15:13 NLT). Through his sacrificial death on our behalf, Jesus proved the depth of his love and commitment to his friends.

May you find the freedom to be completely yourself with God.

In the significant and mundane, Christ beckons you to trust him.

God doesn't want your obedience out of obligation, guilt, or fear, but seeks your friendship.

May you open yourself to Jesus vulnerably, for God is safe, trustworthy, and kind.

In your friendship with God, may you experience the joy of knowing and being known, of loving and being loved, of giving and receiving.

With God, feel the healing joy of loving and being loved in return.

Jesus, thank you for seeking me out as a friend. I'm in awe that you see me not only as a citizen of your kingdom but as a friend.

DAY 95

Wonder at the World

Surely I spoke of things I did not understand,
things too wonderful for me to know. (Job 42:3)

The whole earth is filled with awe at your wonders;
where morning dawns, where evening fades,
you call forth songs of joy. (Psalm 65:8)

May you open your eyes to delight and your heart to
wonder.

Let yourself be amazed by the astonishing beauty of the
Creator's world.

May your past not embitter you from tasting the sweetness
of gratitude and the freshness of joy.

Despite your regrets and mistakes, may you yet open the
window of your heart to bright hope, endless curiosity, and
infinite love.

May you trust in the power of forgiveness and the freedom of Christ's redemption.

Whatever challenges and confusion may exist in your past or present circumstances, may you look up and revive your spirit:

God delights in the opportunity to surprise you!

Jesus, may I never forget to be in awe of the beauty of creation. I am astonished by the works of your hands.

DAY 96

The Lord Watches over You

The LORD watches over you—
　　the LORD is your shade at your right hand;
the sun will not harm you by day,
　　nor the moon by night. (Psalm 121:5–6)

May the God who sees you watch over your coming and your going.

May the Redeemer guard you from every evil.

May God illuminate your darkness, be your shade in the heat, and sustain and refresh you with his wellspring of provision.

Christ will not let you fall.

You are protected, now and forever.

*God, thank you for watching over me. Help me
trust in your daily protection and provision.*

DAY 97

Joy in the Ordinary

L et them give thanks to the LORD for his unfailing love
        and his wonderful deeds for mankind,
for he satisfies the thirsty
            and fills the hungry with good things.
                (Psalm 107:8–9)

May you wake up to each day's fresh possibility.

Celebrate and savor what makes your senses come alive:
the scent of afternoon rain, the crispness of a Fuji apple, the
string struck expertly on a violin, the belonging felt in the
warmth of a hug.

May you give thanks for the small and the commonplace,
seeing that all are cared for and celebrated by God.

May you make an extra effort to express gratitude to someone today—

to pay forward simple kindness and love.

May you tell the people in your life how much they mean to you.

May you take joy in how much you mean to God.

Jesus, give me eyes to recognize your exquisite gifts—the wonder, joy, and beauty of your creation—as I go about my daily routines and habits.

DAY 98

Physician (*Iatros*)

Jesus answered them, "It is not the healthy who need a doctor, but the sick. I have not come to call the righteous, but sinners to repentance." (Luke 5:31–32)

- -

PHYSICIAN (*Iatros*). At the start of his ministry, Jesus describes his mission as being that of a physician (Luke 4:16–24). Jesus is the Great Physician. While he walked the earth, Jesus regularly healed and delivered people emotionally, spiritually, and physically, even raising several from the dead. Through Jesus's death and resurrection, he healed us from our sins and delivered us from spiritual death. Isaiah prophesied that "by his wounds we are healed" (Isaiah 53:5).

- -

May the God of all comfort revive you emotionally, mentally, physically, and spiritually.

May your bondage—to worry, fear, and perfectionism—be undone.

Instead of listening to the enemy's lies, may you turn your eyes to your Great Physician.

May God's healing love release you from toxic mindsets, hopelessness, and attitudes that diminish and discourage you. May you be filled instead with renewed peace, well-being, and ongoing stability.

Today, may you awaken your courage, revive your hope, and open your heart to the life-giving power of the Healer's work in you.

Jesus, may you revive and restore every area of my life with your cleansing power and love. Free me from anything keeping me from fully enjoying you and living in truth.

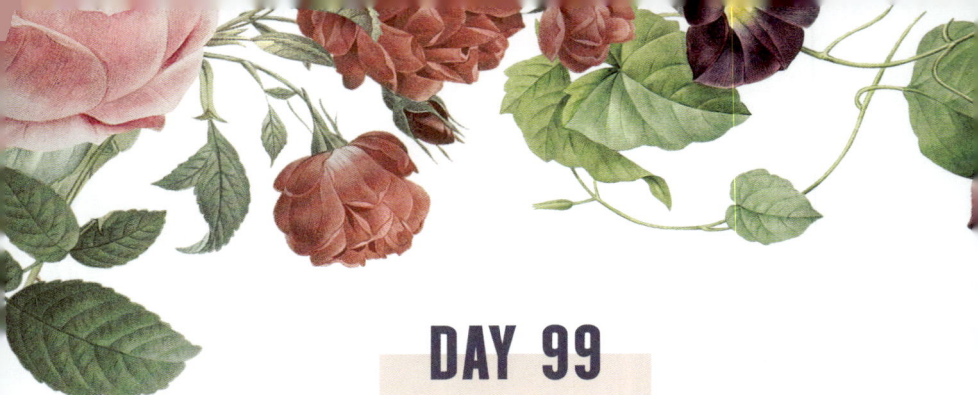

DAY 99

For the Journey

He refreshes my soul. (Psalm 23:3)

. . . .

You've walked a long way. Your feet are tired and worn from the journey.

In spite of your fatigue, may you take the next step.

May you find that you've had a Companion all along—walking beside you, protecting you, guiding you, his shepherd's staff in hand.

May his calming reassurance and life-giving mercy trail you lifelong.

No matter the length of the journey or the hazards or perils of the road, your Companion will get you safely home.

Meanwhile, may you allow the Good Shepherd to refresh and nourish your soul, to uplift your spirit and replenish your joy.

Everything you need can be found in him.

Good Shepherd, during weary, lonely days, help me to find my footing. Thank you for giving me strength for the next step and deep joy for whatever lies ahead.

DAY 100

Stay Open to Surprise

In the morning, O LORD, You will hear my voice;
In the morning I will prepare [a prayer and a sacrifice]
      for You and watch and wait [for You to speak to my
         heart]. (Psalm 5:3 AMP)

Each morning brings a fresh invitation knocking at your door:

a brand-new possibility; a challenge, a joy;
the chance to rely on God or renew your courage.

May you risk going beyond your safe routines and habits to welcome this unexpected guest.

Dare to rise up to greet this visitor with curiosity and wonder instead of fear.

Clean out your rooms, let your soul's windows open wide, and make plenty of space. Make room in your heart for this fresh possibility.

Though unforeseen to you, each day's invitations are antici-
pated, cared for, by God.

Today, may you stay open to God's every gift and surprise.

*God, each day something new comes knocking at
my door. Help me not to ignore this new possibility
by clinging to the familiar or routine, but give
me the ability to stay open to your surprises.*

Permissions